SIMON B⊢

Reframing Marketing

A 3-step plan for effective and ethical marketing for coaches, consultants and freelancers

Katherine
Enjoy the book.
Happy Marketing!
Simon

Contents

Resources

The supporting templates for this book can be found at:

reframingmarketing.com

On my website you will find more content, guides and courses that expand on the ideas in this book. You can also find out how to work with Simon 1-2-1 and book them as a guest or speaker.

simonbatchelar.co.uk

Foreword - Why do we need to reframe marketing?

There is a common belief in marketing and advertising that the only or best way to 'sell what you do' is to use psychological manipulation. Selling people things they don't need, tricking people into buying things they don't want, supports and feeds a system of over-consumption, oppression and inequality.

Many unethical marketing practices have become normalised and accepted by consumers. By bombarding people with advertising and demanding their attention, people have become blind to the presence of advertising in many areas of life.

It's nonsense and it doesn't have to be this way. In this book I will explain why I think this and offer an alternative.

Current marketing thinking is a hangover from the industrial era, focused on grabbing attention, creating urgency and pushing for a sale. Most current business and media platforms (both online and offline) are based on this model. While there are signs of change, the norm is still to interrupt your attention with paid ads or make you pay to skip those ads.

Many of today's household brands were originally built using manipulative advertising. Ethics didn't matter - sales did. And as we know, history is written by the winners, so we only hear about these 'winning' tactics.

This leads to the (false) idea that the only way to sell successfully is to manipulate.

There is an alternative: to market more ethically. Today, purchases are increasingly values-based, as consumers become more aware of the ethics of the brands they choose to buy. Slowly but surely, the age of mass surveillance advertising is coming to an end and the ethics of brands and how they are marketed is a critical factor in their success.

People are afraid to be the first to stop doing what they think is working for their competitors. After all, if your advertising works, you might make enough money to buy more advertising. The question people seem to be afraid to ask is, "What would happen if we stopped marketing like this?"

Your choice of marketing strategies and tactics is important. It's about much more than what kind of ads to run. Like it or not, your marketing speaks volumes, both about what you're selling and about you: your values, your principles, how you see and engage with the world, your brand.

Yes, the win-at-all-costs approach sounds tempting - it's meant to be. There's a lot of money to be made by convincing people that they need to 'out-advertise' the competition. The system relies on the fear that you need to buy more ads than your competitors or do a huge sale on Black Friday, leveraging the fear of missing out to avoid being left behind.

The problem is that this kind of ego-driven, bulldozer marketing is what got us where we are today. Desperately manipulating each other as we race towards disaster (environmental and otherwise).

Having worked in marketing for over 20 years, I know how easy it is to throw money at Google, Meta and the rest and hope that their 'magic ad machine' will produce the promised clients.

It's not that this approach doesn't work, it's just that it perpetuates the world we have - and that's not sustainable.

I believe the alternative is marketing that is more ethical. If we choose to make ethical choices in the way we live our lives and run our businesses, the large-scale change the world needs will be easier for everyone.

That sounds great, it also sounds difficult, and it is. Some of us can change, and it's up to us to do it for those who can't (yet). I'm less concerned with finding out who can and who can't - I want to show you a path to change that you can take when you're ready.

And yes, I know I'm coming from a very privileged position. We don't all start from the same place and change is easier for me than for many others. The world is neither fair or equal - I hope we can do the work to change that, together.

I also know that there are many people who are willing and able to make a change, big or small. It all counts because individual change drives collective action.

There are a lot of areas that I don't cover in this book. Not because they aren't important but because they have been written about before or are still developing, and more importantly, they are not my conversations to represent. Instead, I am committed to making space for and actively seeking out conversations I might not otherwise have had or been involved in, to learn and listen.

I believe that marketing can and should be both effective and ethical.

The aim of this book is to offer my perspective and insights, sharing a 3-step process that will show you how to connect with new clients who are ready to work with you. Hopefully, this will inspire others to bring their own perspectives and conversations to the table.

The tide is turning in how people think about and approach marketing. Together we have an amazing opportunity to create a new and better way of engaging with our clients.

Terms used in this book

Audience: this is the wider group of people who you are addressing. Some of them know you, some of them don't. Anyone who will potentially see your marketing materials is in your audience.

Prospective clients: these are people who like what you do and the way you talk about it. They regularly engage with your content and are curious to find out more.

Client: this is someone who has said yes to working with you in some capacity. I also include in this people who buy a 'product' like a book or a course.

The work: this term is used to describe the activity involved in delivering the outcomes, insights or ideas that you promise to the client.

Paid ads or Ads: this refers to paid-for advertising, both online with Google, Meta, TikTok, etc. and in traditional media, like a newspaper or magazine.

These terms will become a lot clearer as we go through the book.

I

A fresh perspective on marketing

"Because marketing has been done to us for so long we take it for granted. Like the fish who doesn't understand water, we fail to see what's actually happening and don't notice how it's changing us."

Seth Godin

1

Be yourself - and get paid for it

If you've picked up this book (or are looking at a preview online) because you're looking for a new approach to marketing yourself, then I think we have a lot in common.

You're in the right place.

If you see yourself as a coach, consultant, freelancer, solopreneur, thought leader or personal brand then this book is for you.

In it, I describe a 3-step plan for effective and ethical marketing. It will show you how to do what you do best, create the change you want to inspire, make or lead, and get paid for it.

Although marketing is simple, it's not always easy. That's why I'm sharing this manageable plan that avoids the worst aspects of marketing and offers an alternative perspective based on connection rather than manipulation.

I am not claiming that this book will make you a millionaire (unlike some others). I'm not here to make false promises or try to tell you what to do. I don't claim to be a 'marketing guru'. I see myself as a guide who wants to share with you the insights I've gained from 20 years of running a marketing agency, and working with hundreds of people just like you.

If you're looking for a shortcut or a list of 10 things to do that will *guarantee* you more clients or money, then this is not the book for you. There are plenty of people out there who will make those promises, take your money and then explain why it's your fault it didn't work.

When it comes to marketing, I don't believe in tick-box lists or quick fixes that work for everyone, every time. Marketing is more personal than that.

My aim is to present an alternative way of marketing that allows you to find your own solutions, connect with new people, do your best work, and make a difference in the world.

I like to think of this book as a map showing a clear path, with some important waypoints marked en route. The actual path you take will be different from mine, and from everyone else reading this book. Where you start, how long it takes and exactly where you end up is up to you.

Whatever your starting point, the aim of this book is the same: to package your best work, take it to the people who will benefit most from it, and invite them to work with you in an ethical and effective way.

2

Are you willing to change?

Many of you will be reading this book because your marketing isn't working or doesn't feel right. I've been there too, so this isn't a judgement, it's an acknowledgement.

It's OK to realise that you're on the wrong track, or that you're a little lost, or even that you feel like giving up completely. I would bet that every person in business has felt this way at some point - I certainly have over the years - not many people talk about it.

If what you're doing isn't working, more of the same isn't the answer.

It's time to try something different, and that's what this book is about.

It's not a book of answers, it's not the only way, and it's certainly not the last word. It is an alternative perspective, based on my experience and learning, which I hope will inspire, motivate and empower you to make a difference in your world through your work.

Fair warning, though: the only way you are going to get different results is by doing things differently. This book will suggest some different ways of thinking, doing and being. There will be many invitations to try something new.

Be brave and try them.

After all, you picked up this book because you're open to alternative ideas, because you want to reframe your marketing.

So let's get started.

3

Marketing vs. advertising

Before we go any further, I'd like to make a distinction between marketing and advertising. Most people think of marketing as advertising - but they are different.

Marketing is part of your strategy to achieve a goal that you have set. Marketing is a collection of activities that you believe will get you closer to where you want to be.

Advertising is one tactic of marketing. Advertising comes in many formats and takes many forms.

So, advertising is part of a marketing strategy. From conversations with business owners, many of them think, and are regularly told, that advertising is the strategy. When in fact it is only one part of it.

4

What's wrong with marketing today?

Alice Karolina, the founder of The Ethical Move, summarised traditional marketing perfectly in one of her blog posts:

*"By placing shame, fear, and fake needs into our minds every second of
every day, psychological tactics are made to bypass our decision-making
process — using our brains against us to make a profit."*[1]

I don't want to dwell too long on the problems with marketing. Rather
than spending time on the negatives, this book is all about the positive
actions you can take. That said, I think it is useful to quickly look at
some of the current issues so we can ensure we avoid them, or at least
are aware of them when we start thinking about how you are going to
market more ethically.

---

[1]   Alice Karolina, The Big Picture of Ethical Marketing, Medium: https://medium.com/t
      he-ethical-move/the-big-picture-of-ethical-marketing-705eac9ee9e

Demanding attention

Modern advertising is an interruption of what people actually want. The people you are trying to reach are increasingly wary, inundated and exhausted by it. When advertising works, the recipient rewards you with their attention - a price that fewer and fewer people are willing to pay. We each only have a limited amount of attention, and we choose where to focus it. People pay attention to things they're interested in. People don't generally appreciate having their attention hijacked.

Manipulation

This is what happens when you act from a position of power, with more knowledge and insight, to coerce or encourage people into doing something they regret. This often takes the form of generating false needs - convincing someone of something that is not true. Manipulation works through the creation or exaggeration of a fear of failure or loss. Often resulting in selling people things they don't need. This is what causes buyer's remorse.

Unnecessary pressure

Adding pressure to a decision is one of the most common techniques I see in marketing and sales. It often involves arbitrary deadlines, countdown timers or 'we've got someone else ready to buy' techniques. They are psychologically researched and often used with weaponised effectiveness. The question people are afraid to ask is: if you have to rely on manipulating someone into buying, are they a good client?

False scarcity

In many cases, there is a limited number or capacity that determines the availability of what you are selling. For example, 30 tickets for your event (with 30 seats). Where it becomes problematic is when people use false scarcity. For example, saying, "Only two places left," when in fact there are many more. Sometimes the whole marketing campaign seems to be about selling the 'last few places'!

Reciprocity

What is reciprocity? It's defined as, *"the practice of exchanging things with others for mutual benefit."*[2] What this means is that if you give someone something, they will in some way feel the need to give you something in return, or repay you in some way. This happens without conscious thought. It's just the way they're likely to feel: indebted to you. This may well be an unintended result of your actions. There are ways in which you can still give people something and minimise the reciprocity factor, and we will look at these later in the book.

Status and shame

Our perceived status is relative and there are different levels of status among our friends, family and community. There is your external status, how you are perceived by others, and your internal status, how you see yourself. Whether you like it or not, you care about your status, and you are always calculating your own status.

We are constantly looking at others to assess where we stand on the status scale. Not everyone wants to raise their status. Some do, but

---

[2]   Wikipedia: https://simple.wikipedia.org/wiki/Reciprocity_(cultural_anthropology)

most people are happy where they are, they just don't want to move down too far. Others have been conditioned to believe that they are of a certain status and will fight to stay where they are. Some people use status against us in their marketing because they understand that deep down we care.

By making people angry and frustrated with their current status, you can get them to buy things they don't need. Even if they have enough, you can play on people's insecurities and make them want to earn more status for themselves. By creating and then exploiting 'false needs' such as fame, body image or perceived wealth, you can create a fear of shame while emphasising the allure of status.

Shame, a basic human emotion along with happiness and fear, is the status enforcer. When we are surrounded by people we perceive as having more status than we do, we feel shame. And people fear shame.

"Shame undermines all of the things we seek to have. So to avoid shame, we make bad decisions, ones that honour marketers or those who seek to manipulate us, as opposed to doing what is best for us, and the people around us."[3]

It is this link between status and shame that can motivate people to act, to buy. Status only works when it is enforced by shame.

It's not always out in the open, it's mostly in our heads, it's the story we tell ourselves about our work and how we're judged. Marketers know that status always works, all they have to do is highlight it and gently (and in some cases not so gently) remind us that we don't want to be 'low status', we don't want to experience shame.

---

[3] AKIMBO podcast - Seth Godin - Status roles https://open.spotify.com/episode/2MCl
RZNlDFDqXmi32H21f7?si=OdznSupqQ_2BMXns_NWOwg

Luxury goods give people a way to publicly display their status, to impress others, and perhaps even to shame them. Online digital platforms give us virtual status in the form of vanity metrics such as followers, likes or views. The platforms trade off the constant shifting of status - some move up, others move down - and rely on status-related shame to create a hierarchy of rank and pecking order.

Is there another way?

It can feel like there's a lot of pressure to do your marketing a certain way. As James Clear says, *"Most days we'd rather be wrong with the crowd rather than right by ourselves."*[4] So, I offer an alternative way of thinking about and doing your marketing.

It's easier to choose an alternative way of marketing when it's just you. You are free to be creative and true to yourself because you don't have to satisfy the interests of investors and shareholders.

When you use a more ethical marketing strategy and tactics, you attract clients who are ready to work with you. When you're open about what you're offering and why, you're not trying to trick or pressure anyone into buying. This means that the work you do is much more likely to be effective and appreciated.

This is you making a difference. Without manipulation. That's what the world needs right now: more people who make a difference, who inspire, teach, motivate and change perspectives, as well as those who are forgiving, accepting, understanding and empathising.

---

[4] James Clear, Atomic Habits, Random House Business Books 2018, 121

When you have that impact on one client, they are more likely to refer others to you, which leads to you having an impact on more people. And so the cycle continues and the impact grows and grows.

What's more, the people you work with may be inspired by you - to change their perspective, to look for ways to make a difference in the world. Your ethics and marketing lead by example and the ripples spread outwards, into society.

Earlier I mentioned people who are not yet ready to make the shift to more ethical marketing and behaviour. When others see an ethical stance working for you, it can be just the catalyst they need to take action themselves.

So let's make a difference.

5

What's a more ethical marketing alternative?

The three things clients want to know

Marketing has three core elements: who, what and why. These elements can be looked at from two perspectives: your perspective, as the person doing the marketing, and the client's perspective.

From the client's perspective, they want to know *who* are the kind of people you work with, *what* you work on with them, and *why* they can trust you to deliver.

Who

Firstly, clients want to understand if you work with people like them. Are you the kind of person who can help them? Are they in the right place? Are they talking to the right person?

They ask: "Who are you working with, are they people like me?"

What?

Next they want to understand what you do and whether it fits with what they're looking for. Are the problems you solve or the changes you help people make something they want to work on?

From the client's perspective, they need to feel they understand what you're doing before they can feel confident enough to believe it's right for them.

They ask: "Is this what I am looking for?"

Why

Finally, before they say yes, they're trying to determine if they feel ready to fully commit to the process and the work.

They ask: "Why should I trust this person to deliver on their promise?"

Your own perspective on the *who, what* and *why* of what you deliver may be different to that of the client- it's likely you know more than them. Part of marketing more ethically is showing empathy, and understanding that the client's perspective is important. Not simply trying to explain why they're wrong and how you can make it right.

As you work through this book, you'll answer these three questions that people ask and base their decisions on. In doing so, you will help prospective clients move through a 3-step journey of connecting, considering and committing.

Your perspective:

Connect

The first step is to connect with people. You want to help them link what they're feeling, thinking and doing now with what they want to feel, think and do in the future. This stage is about helping them to understand more about where they are now and to put into context where they want to be and why they want to be there.

This first stage creates a friendly tension - more like stretching a rubber band rather than a bungee jump. The tension you create here is: "I want to know more". It creates tension in the sense of wanting to know what is possible.

Consider

Next, you give those who want to learn more something to consider, releasing some of the tension you've built up. You show them how where they are now is connected to where they want to be, with a path in between that they can follow. You show them that there is an achievable path between these two places.

At any point, someone can decide it's not for them and drift away. That's the great thing about friendly tension: it motivates those who resonate with what you're offering. For those who don't, they're not trapped, deceived or manipulated - they're free to 'leave' and connect and consider elsewhere.

Commit

The final stage is to invite them to commit. This is where you offer to guide them through the process you outlined in the Consider stage. The change they can make with your guidance from where they are now to where they want to be. This is where you set out the promise you're making and make clear the commitment of time, energy and money needed to get there. Once someone has decided they're ready to commit, you make the first step as easy as possible and explain clearly what happens next.

In making this invitation, you're offering to release the tension completely.

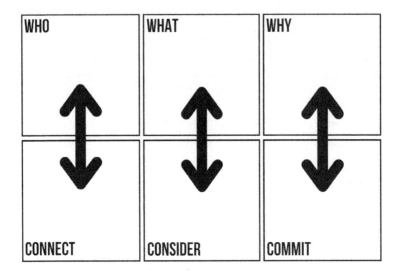

Putting it all together

To answer the three things the client wants to understand - the *who*, *what* and *why* - your marketing should follow the connect, consider and commit structure.

There are some simple things you can do at each stage. We'll go into much more detail in the next few chapters. For now it's important to illustrate how marketing activities are used in this process.

When you take the three stages - Connect, Consider, Commit - and combine them with your *who*, *what* and *why*, you build a simple and effective 3-step marketing process[5].

---

[5] This process is inspired by Eugene Schwartz's 5 levels of awareness, from his book Breakthrough Advertising published in 1966. The 5 levels are explained in more detail in the appendix of this book if you want to learn more.

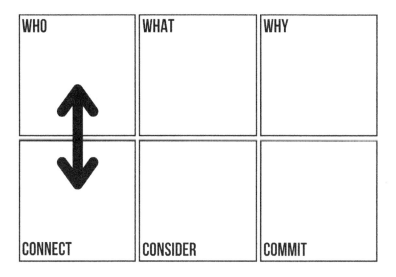

Who + Connect

This is where you identify your audience, the people whose attention you want to attract, and connect with them using empathy and authority, showing them what's possible.

The more clearly you articulate your *who*, the easier it is for people to connect because they will think, "That sounds like where I am right now." This will naturally create some tension as they begin to see an opportunity for change, and start to think about where they might end up. This tension will motivate them to discover more.

This stage lends itself well to social media, YouTube, podcasts and networking. It's simply about making connections, throwing out ideas, offering different perspectives on the narrative or challenging 'status quo' thinking. Your aim is to get people thinking, create that friendly tension and point them in the direction of where they can find out more.

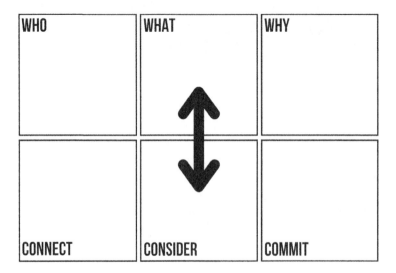

What + Consider

Once people have made the connection and want to know more, you can help them understand what they're looking for in greater depth.

This is where you show them that you understand where they are now and that what you deliver links them to where they want to be. Maybe they want to make a change, do something differently, start doing something new or stop doing something. You can help them understand what might be stopping them from starting or doing this on their own.

This is where you give them something to consider. The key is that this is NOT your product. It's not about making a sale, it's just about deepening their understanding of how where they are now is linked to where they want to be.

This stage is focused on helping people decide if where they think they want to end up is right for them. Spending time and effort helping people deepen their understanding at this stage, whilst not selling, feels counterproductive to some. The reason it is worthwhile is that once someone has decided that they want something, it's very hard to change their mind, and it's also much easier for them to see the value in getting what they want.

By not talking about what you deliver or focusing on the sale too early and instead talking about what it will be like *after* you have delivered, you are helping people decide for themselves if what you are delivering is what they really want.

You'll release some tension by showing them what they can do to get where they want to be, and then create a bit more as they realise they may need someone or something to get them there.

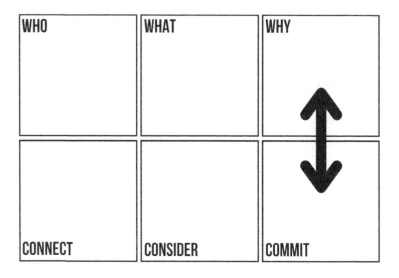

Why + Commit

This is where you set out the promise you're making. It's where you explain what change you are going to help them make, when they will get there and what commitment you need from them. This could be time, energy or money.

When someone is clear on where they want to go, and why they want to go there, you often don't have to 'make a sale' because all they need to see is your promise to guide them in making this change.

The idea is to separate the sale from the consideration. This means that people can understand and contextualise what they are buying before they are asked to make a decision about buying it. So the people who are ready to commit really want to take that first step because they are ready to do the work and make the change they are seeking. All you need to do is make the first step clear and simple.

When you are clear on who you want to connect with, you will attract those who are motivated to consider what you are offering. For those who feel ready to commit to the work they will be clear on why they can trust you to guide them.

6

Using tension, not manipulation

Why does reframing marketing work? How does taking a prospect through the connect-consider-commit journey lead them to become an actual client?

The answer is the tension you create along the way.

Tension means different things to different people. It is used in films and television to build suspense and keep you guessing.

For me, tension is not the same as fear. Fear underpins all the tactics we've discussed that are wrong in marketing, using pressure and manipulation.

More ethical marketing does something different, it creates tension. Not the uncomfortable tension of a thriller, more like the tension of stretching a rubber band. The purpose of tension is not to apply pressure, it's to create forward movement, to create a sense of what is possible, what can be achieved, what change can be made.

"For most of us changing our behaviour is driven by our desire to fit in and our perception of our status. Since both of these forces often push us to stay as we are, it takes tension to change them."[6]

When we talk to our audience with empathy about where they are now and where they would like to be, we show them that change is possible. Change is something that disrupts the daily routine or the tried and tested way of doing things. Sometimes it is a life event, a shift in perspective or a sudden insight. Most of the time we go about our day without change occurring (or at least, we don't notice it). When it does happen, tension is created and we can choose to be open to exploring that change.

"Provide the kind of tension that can only be released by being willing to change."[7]

When we market ethically, we give the client everything they need to decide for themselves whether they are willing to do the work to make a change.

The tension we create in our marketing is a signal to those who feel they're ready: to take action, to learn more, and to make a change.

That said, it's very common for people to be afraid of trying something new. After all, you don't know how to do a new thing until you do it. With the right guidance and enough practice, the thing we were afraid to do often becomes easy or even second nature. The tension we create in our marketing feels the same.

---

[6]   Seth Godin, This Is Marketing, Penguin Business 2018, 103

[7]   Seth Godin, This Is Marketing, Penguin Business 2018, 115

As I said at the beginning of this chapter, marketing is simple, just not always easy. As I hope you can see, the process is straightforward - just these three steps: connect, consider, commit. Next we'll look at how to build these three steps into a marketing plan.

7

You're not for everyone and that's ok

The last point I want to make before we start planning may seem a little strange: for the vast majority of people, what you're doing is simply not right for them, and they will have little or no interest in what you're offering.

This is a good thing!

As Seth Godin says:

"You'll never be able to serve everyone, which is comforting since you're less likely to be disappointed when it doesn't happen."[8]

Trying to sell to people you're not right for is exhausting, and isn't exactly ethical.

For your marketing to be both effective and more ethical, it needs to speak to your ideal client (we'll work on who they are in the next few

---

[8]   This is a phrase that Seth often says on his podcasts, but it isn't found in his books.

chapters). By not trying to appeal to the widest possible audience, you will save a lot of time and energy and ensure that your marketing is far more effective.

8

Cascade of clients

It can feel like you need to rush ahead with your marketing and try to get people to buy what you're selling, now. A lot of marketing advice I see is focused on getting people to the sale as quickly as possible.

Whilst working with a new client is definitely the aim of your marketing, what you want to avoid is getting a lot of clients who are not ready to do the work, will not commit to the process, or are unlikely to feel the benefits of working with you. This is what happens when you rush ahead with your marketing, you don't give people time to consider what you're offering.

Rushed marketing often relies on closing the sale, and leaving your natural position in order to 'win' the client, which can feel in conflict with your desire to be authentic.

A lot of people don't like the idea of 'selling' and therefore don't like the idea of marketing themselves. There is a particular feeling that arises in people if you talk to them about 'making a sale'; and I would say that for most people it's not a feeling they like. It can be even less appealing when what you are selling is the work *you* do.

The way we're going to approach marketing doesn't focus on the selling bit of sales. It's more like not trying to sell anything and I find it feels a lot better for the seller, and when a sale is made, the client is delighted.

Instead of a sales pitch, offer them a journey

This 'non-selling' sales technique is not quick and that's why it works so well for considered purchases. The idea is to focus on the questions the client may have, then answer those questions to guide them to a point where they understand what change they want to make, they trust you to deliver on your promises, and they want to know when they can start.

The process is like a journey that the client goes on:

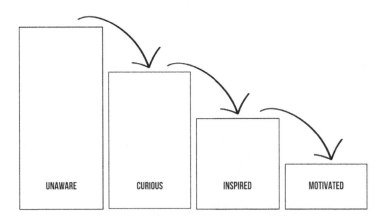

Unaware: They begin by being unaware that there is something in their life that they might like to change, either personally or in their business. This could be an action, feeling, thought or process they are repeating. This is how most people are most of the time.

Curious: At some point they become aware that this thing in their life is something that is connected to another way of being and they are curious to find out more. By this I mean they see an opportunity for change, they start to feel that change is possible.

Inspired: At this point they feel inspired to find out more about this change and how they might shift from where they are now to this new desirable state. Their questions tend to focus on what the process of change involves and how much effort, investment and time it will take.

Motivated: At this point, they are likely to be motivated to look for someone to guide them in making this change, someone who knows the process and has guided others before.

Ethical marketing is all about providing what the client is looking for throughout this journey. This is how you sell without selling.

At the *Connect* stage, you will create content and show up in places where your ideal client is looking for answers to connect with people who are curious about change.

In the *Consider* stage, you will explain the change that is possible and inspire the people who feel that this is the change they are seeking.

In the *Commit* stage you will offer to guide the people who are motivated to make the change.

The marketing journey itself attracts the clients you're looking for, without needing a sales pitch or special offer or 'opportunity of a lifetime'. In doing so, you will end up talking to people who are ready to do the work involved and are ready to invest in making their change happen. You're not 'selling', you're being authentic.

Using this plan, you'll set up the journey and then act as a guide for those who want to know, explore and discover more.

Now let's start creating your 3-step plan.

II

Making Your Marketing Plan

Marketing is simple, not always easy.

9

The simple 6 box plan

The process of creating a marketing plan that attracts and retains your ideal clients is reassuringly simple. It's made up of the six elements from the previous chapter. It won't surprise you that I've called it the 6-box plan.

WHO	WHAT	WHY
CONNECT	CONSIDER	COMMIT

The first three boxes deal with the questions people are asking: *who*, *what* and *why*. In the next three chapters, we'll spend some time looking at these questions to understand why they are asking them and what they're looking for in your answers. This will enable us to build the next three boxes of the plan: connect, consider and commit.

To put this into practice and build a journey for people to go on, we need to start at the end. This may seem counterintuitive as it is the opposite of how your clients will experience the journey.

To understand why this order makes sense, imagine you're trying to persuade someone to climb a mountain with you. If you start where the client starts, you'll be at the bottom of the mountain asking people if they want you to lead them to the top. Their first questions might be, "What's it like at the top?" and, "How long does it take to get there?"

If you haven't made a map for them to look at, and you don't have a picture or description of what it's like at the top, then you don't have any answers to these questions. You're asking them to take a huge leap of faith.

Now consider this the other way round. If you've already been to the top, taken some photos and made a map of how you climbed the mountain, you have the answers to their questions. When you stand at the bottom and ask people if they want you to guide them to the top of the mountain, you can show them the pictures and the map. Now they know what they're getting into.

In this way, the end of the journey is actually the best place to start. It means you're setting up signposts for people to follow all along the way. In marketing terms, if you already have a place for the person to commit to, and you have all the things that they need to consider, then you can focus your creative energy on the connect step.

Over the next nine chapters we'll work through each of the six boxes, completing them as you go. We start with the *who, what* and *why.* These will flow logically from the understanding you already have, or will work to gain, of the prospective client's situation. We then work on the basics of method, product, and price before moving on to look at the Commit stage, followed by Consider and then Connect.

From this you can create a short (manageable) marketing campaign. That might sound big and complicated, it's actually the opposite. Each campaign is just a series of pieces of content you create with the intention of achieving an outcome. So you can set up a campaign to get your next six 1-2-1 clients, or a campaign to launch your latest course. The plan you're about to create will give you all the tools you need to set up these campaigns easily and make the process of marketing feel simpler and, I hope, more enjoyable.

I have created a simple 6-box plan template that you can download for free from the Reframing Marketing website, just go to:

reframingmarketing.com/downloads

A quick note about taking notes... You can of course make your own notes in your own style, either digitally or on paper, whatever works for you. As those of you who have seen videos on my YouTube channel[9] will know, I personally prefer flipchart. The boxes are just a neat way of illustrating the sections for the book, you can use circles, ovals or even make a list.

---

9   https://www.youtube.com/@simonbatchelar

III

Who - What - Why

Clients want to know who are the kind of people you work with, what you work on with them, and why they can trust you to deliver.

10

BOX 1: Who is it for?

WHO ★	WHAT	WHY
CONNECT	CONSIDER	COMMIT

First, we'll look at the audience for your marketing: who you want to work with, and therefore who you want to connect with. I'll refer to them as your *who*.

By the end of this chapter, you will be able to answer these three questions:

- Who is your ideal client?
- What is their worldview?
- Where do you find them?

Your *who* is often referred to as your 'niche', and is something that many people think they have but in reality many are not brave enough to commit to. Having a niche doesn't necessarily mean having a 'customer persona' or a list of hyper-specific demographics. Sometimes it's easier to view it as the answer to the question: who is your work for?

One thing is true, there is no business where you can say, "Everyone is my client," that just can't be true. That would mean that you can effectively deliver results for babies, toddlers, teenagers, adults and seniors, no matter where they come from or what they want to achieve. That's 7.5 billion people. Not even a mega-brand like Coca-Cola can say that. Simply by narrowing it down to people who like sweet fizzy drinks, already, it's clearly not for a huge section of the global population.

11

Who are you making change happen for?

The concept of making change happen for your clients may be very clear, it may feel a little tenuous. The reason I focus on making change happen is because once you understand and can articulate what change your client is experiencing, your marketing becomes much easier. We'll take a closer look at this change in the next section. First, let's look at who you are trying to create change for.

A lot of industrial era marketing focuses on demographics - what people look like, what they do and where they live. If you are doing high-level brand awareness marketing - simply getting your brand in front of people - this way of thinking about people can be useful and effective.

However, brand awareness marketing is almost impossible to link to sales and is really just about getting your brand seen enough times before someone makes a transactional level purchase or search online so that there is a chance they will choose your brand or click on your link instead of your main competitor. For big brands, this is simply a cost of doing business. They have to spend hundreds of thousands, if not millions, a year just to get people to remember their name.

The vast majority of businesses don't need to do this level of marketing.

Instead, it's far more effective to focus on psychographics - what people like, want, believe and do.

The way you talk about your *who* defines the rest of your marketing, so it's really important to spend time on this before moving on. You can always refine and develop your *who*, it will become more and more detailed over time. It's fine to start broad, but not too broad (there's an exercise coming up to help with this).

The next sections are different ways to get clever on your *who*. Some of these may not feel right or may be something you can answer very easily. I suggest you work through each one and at the end we'll bring all those ideas together.

12

What is their worldview?

When thinking about and describing your *who*, the best place to start is people's worldview. We want to market to people based on what they believe, dream, and want. It is less important to consider what they look like or how they present themselves. In marketing terms, this means using psychographics over demographics.

Demographics used to be how marketers divided up the world. For a time this worked. You could buy lists of housewives, or accountants and sell these people things based on assumptions you made about their lives. Facebook (now Meta) took this to the extreme and was able to break down people's demographics into a baffling array of ways to target people based on data it stole from their online behaviours. In today's world, and the coming world, these demographics are less and less effective as the world of work and life is changing beyond neat silos of behaviour.

Demographics are based on observable traits like age and income, while psychographics focus on beliefs, desires, and behaviors. Effective and ethical marketing identifies and creates anticipated, personal and relevant marketing messages for specific groups sharing common psychographics.

While everyone is an individual and everyone can show up how they choose, marketing to one person at a time is a daunting prospect. Luckily, as humans, we overlap in areas where we share a worldview, as theorised by George Lakoff, and this is where we can begin to talk to more than one person at a time.

"A worldview is a collection of attitudes, values, stories and expectations about the world around us which inform our every thought and action. Worldview is expressed in ethics, religion, philosophy, scientific beliefs and so on."[10]

Different individuals perceive the world differently based on their beliefs and experiences. It's therefore important to understand and target the right audience in your marketing. Your product or message will not resonate with everyone so it's crucial to focus on those it is intended for.

We'll begin to describe your *who* in the next section.

Who is it not for?

"Saying 'it's not for you' shows the ability to respect someone enough that you're not going to waste their time, pander to them or insist that they change their beliefs. It shows respect for those you seek to serve, to say to them, I made this for you, not for the other folks, but for you."[11]

---

[10] Sire, J. W. (2004) Naming the Elephant: Worldview as a Concept. https://www.ncbi.nl m.nih.gov/pmc/articles/PMC6735033/

[11] Seth Godin, This Is Marketing, Penguin Business 2018, 37

It can be useful to start off by thinking about who you *don't* want to work with. After all, if you are going to be working with these people a lot, plus putting time and energy into marketing to them, then you want to attract the kind of people you want to work with. It has always seemed counterintuitive to me when I meet people who can choose their clients who say they have a lot of clients that frustrate them.

We can minimise this frustration by focusing our marketing on those clients we do want to work with. We can also pass those clients we don't want to work with on to someone else who can serve them better, or point them in the direction of where they might find the change they seek.

Here are three key principles to consider.

- Just because they *could* be a client doesn't mean they *have* to be.
- Just because they *might* need or want what you offer doesn't mean you have you work with them.
- Just because they can or want to pay you doesn't mean you *have* to accept.

EXERCISE: What do they believe?

Thinking about your ideal client and their worldview, can you describe in broad terms some of their attitudes, values, stories and expectations about the world?

From this, are you able to identify people with whom you do *not* wish to work?

It's ok if, at this stage, a set of values or attitudes arises without which a person is unlikely to be a good fit for working with you.

For example, people who resonate with my work often have a worldview that is different from the mainstream. They like to do things their own way, not at the expense of people or the planet. From this, I am able to say that I don't want to work with people who are driven only by money and are willing to win at all costs. Although this isn't particularly specific, it saves me a lot of time and energy knowing that I don't have to write or create content for these people or listen too closely to what they think of what I share.

Another example might be people who have reached a point in their lives where they want to invest more in themselves - perhaps their fitness or self-development. They want to make changes and are seeking guidance on what to change and how to make those changes last.

Consider someone who has started their own business and had their first successful year. They now find themselves needing to expand and are not sure how to go about it. They've gotten this far on their own so accepting that they need help is a big step.

The challenge is to define a *who* that effectively captures the commonalities among different individuals while recognising their uniqueness.

13

Who is your ideal client?

When you start out, there will be an aspect of having to say yes to clients who, it later turns out, are not a good fit. That's part of the process. It's unlikely you will settle on exactly who you really enjoy working with straight away. It will take some time, some trial and error and some persistence to really learn who it is, and what it is about them that really works well.

"We can group people into stereotype groups that often (but not always) tell themselves similar stories [and] make similar decisions based on their perceived status and other needs."[12]

Your work isn't going to be for everybody, and there will be some who will get more out of it, or will find working with you easier, simpler, or just get more from the process. This will take time to learn and understand, and even longer to be able to tell this about someone before they become a client.

---

[12] Seth Godin, This Is Marketing, Penguin Business 2018, 14

You won't keep the same *who* forever.

Your *who* will not be chiselled into stone and built into your office wall. It will change, evolve and grow with you over time. You need to start somewhere and even if you have a niche already the following exercise will help you get clearer about who they are and what it is about them that makes them stand out from the crowd.

This exercise is inspired by an activity in a Michael Killen webinar I watched some time ago[13]. It stuck with me and I've used a version of it ever since with my clients.

EXERCISE: Room full of clients

Imagine that I have filled a room with one hundred potential clients – they all say they want what you can help them with.

Now, I want you to select ten of them to work with, the twist being that you will only get paid when they finish their work with you.

Who would you pick from that room full of people? Which ten from the one hundred are better placed for you to help?

There must be some that are a step ahead or in a perfect place to start working with you.

What makes these people stand out?

---

[13] I did look for a link to the webinar recording but I couldn't find it. Thanks for the inspiration, Michael.

Remember that it might not be their job, demographic or income.

It could be their current situation, feelings, emotions or held beliefs. It could be what they're doing, not doing, or whatever is stopping them from doing it.

Sometimes, a great place to start is "someone who thinks X" or "someone who feels Y". Then, add an AND to that thought to narrow down your criteria until you find something you're comfortable with.

Examples:

- Business owners who are scaling their business (broad)
- Business owners who are scaling their business AND have a turnover of £1m (more specific to those who have an idea of their numbers)
- Business owners who are scaling their business AND are feeling out of control (more specific to those who are feeling a certain way)
- Business owners who are scaling their business AND are struggling with their work-life balance (more specific to a time in people's lives)

Spend some time thinking through this. When you think of who you picture as your ideal client, what makes the perfect ones really stand out? This is what narrows your niche and helps you get clear on who you can serve most effectively.

Here are some prompts:

- Is it something they identify with?
- Is it something in their story that unites them?
- Is it a commonality (or difference) between you and them?
- Is it how aware they are of a problem, solution, or outcome?
- Is it how financially (un)stable they are?
- Is it who you can help through them?
- Is it an affinity with something?
- Does a vocation unite them?
- Do they want to work in pairs / teams / alone?
- Do they all aspire to something?
- Is there something in your background, story, qualifications, or vision that you think will resonate?

Make some notes about who you feel stands out before you carry on. We're going to keep working on this so don't worry too much about it being perfect just yet.

14

How to describe your ideal client

Now you have a starting point. If it still feels a bit broad then try adding a *who* to the end and see what comes up. For example:

- Managers. (really wide)
- Managers who have just been promoted. (better)
- Managers who have just been promoted who don't have any previous management experience. (even better)
- Managers who have just been promoted who don't have any previous management experience and who have been given a personal development budget by their boss. (perfect)

You don't have to use this whole description every time you describe who you work with, however the more specific you can be in your mind the better.

An alternative way to think about your niche is to think about how the kind of people you work with think, feel and act. Sometimes your niche could be people who feel a certain way and would like to change the way they feel. Sometimes it can be people who are thinking or believing in a certain idea or concept and would like to shift their perspective.

For example:

- People who run their own business and feel like they've been working on the same thing for years without an end in sight.
- People who have built what they thought was a successful business but is in fact a gilded cage.
- People who struggle to sleep because of the fear of what they have to do at work tomorrow.

Another option is people who are currently doing something which they would either like to stop doing or change. You can of course combine this with a niche that you may have found previously or currently be working with. You can also mix all of these things up.

For example:

- Solopreneurs who add more to their to-do list than they tick off.
- Freelancers who struggle to say no to clients and end up working with people who are draining and demanding.
- People who have an idea for a book but are not sure they can commit to writing it, or don't know where to start.

All these examples are great niches, when people who are feeling, thinking or doing these things read these they think "that's me". You might have thought that yourself reading some of them.

Try adding a *who* to your description(s) from the previous exercise.

15

An easy way to get clear on your niche

Some people say to me, "I don't see the point in defining a niche." They tell me it feels like a lot of effort when they could just be out there doing their work.

There is a common theme among people without a niche: their marketing is happening *despite* them not *because* of them.

For these people, marketing appears to work because for one reason or another it lands in front of people who are ready to buy. They are relying on luck, timing or generosity to find new clients. This is the same as relying on being taken out to lunch every day to feed you. It's great when it happens, you just can't rely on it.

Knowing your niche or your *who* is the most important part of marketing. It's the difference between it working and not.

If you don't know who you're talking to then you can't focus your message, time or energy. It means you end up spending a lot of time and money talking to people who don't want what you offer. It means you have a lot of conversations with people who you think are the right people but they're just not ready to commit, people who aren't ready to see the value in what you do, or have just done what you can help them with. It's exhausting and really frustrating.

Your *who* means you can be confident in the promise you make. It means you can be clear about the change you're going to help them make.

When you tell the story someone has been waiting to hear, they will feel like they have found the perfect person to guide them. They are likely to be a great client who gets a lot out of working with you. Such people really understand the promise you're making.

If the person you talk to isn't the right fit they might know someone who is; and they will feel more confident about referring that someone to you, confident they will be a good fit.

Being able to focus on your *who* also helps when creating content as you don't need to cater to everyone. This saves you a lot of time and energy.

As you can see, the more specific you are the more clients you can get, not less.

Your *who* is for now.

Your *who* will evolve over time and become clearer, and perhaps even change. That's ok. Knowing your *who* gives you a way to focus your marketing messages and content. The more focused you can be about *who* you want to work with, the more effective your marketing will be.

16

Where do you find them?

Another way to get clear on your niche is to think about the kind of places you would find your ideal clients. It also means that when you're looking to connect with them (the Connect stage) you know where to look.

There are three ways to consider your client from this perspective.

1. Where do they spend their time?
2. Who is connected to them, or has them in their audience?
3. Where do they look for answers or information?

EXERCISE: Where do you find them?

Here are some prompts to consider. Write down your answers and if you're not sure or don't know about any of these, that may be something to research further.

- How would you describe the kind of places they spend their time?
- Think about their day to day, are they going to co-working spaces, gyms, sailing clubs, cycling events, independent shops, networking, chamber of commerce meetings, online communities...?
- What kind of people know, work with or are regularly in contact with your *who*?
- Who has an audience of these people already?
- Where do they look for answers or information? Are they using search engines, YouTube, peer networks, experts, coaches?
- Where do they find inspiration? Do they listen to particular podcasts, read certain books, subscribe to specific emails or newsletters?

Looking at your answers, consider:

Can you spend time in these places easily and authentically (i.e. not just showing up to sell things) to get to know them?

If you can't physically or directly be there, can you be there in another way? Can you sponsor or partner with those places? Can you be included in their marketing?

17

WHO BOX

In the WHO box on your marketing plan, write down your description of your ideal client.

If it helps, you can imagine someone has asked you, "Who are the kind of people you work with?" or, "If I am going to refer people to you, who are the kind of people you want me to send your way?"

Also, write down how you would describe their worldview. If this is included in your description above then you can skip this.

18

BOX 2: What value do you deliver?

WHO	WHAT ★	WHY
CONNECT	CONSIDER	COMMIT

Now we're going to get clear on what it is you work on with your clients and how you can articulate this to them in a clear way that makes them curious and excited.

By the end of this chapter, you will be able to answer these questions:

- What do you do?
- Where is your client now?
- Where does your client want to go?
- What's stopping them?
- What are your client's needs and wants?

Are you selling what you want to sell or what they want to buy?

Communicating your *what* is a lot easier if you are clear on your *who*.

If you're not clear on who you want to work with, or buy your course or programme, then you're at risk of selling something you want to sell, rather than selling something your client wants to buy.

Some people have an aversion to the word selling. If that's you, let's reframe that word before we carry on with the help of a quote from Rob Moore:

"Selling is caring enough about someone to discover what is most important to them, and giving it to them."[14]

So, in a way we're all selling, most of the time. We're selling to our friend a choice of restaurant to meet at or to our toddler on why it's bedtime.

When you are 'selling' it's easy to confuse a great idea with something that is actually of value to the client.

---

[14] Rob Moore, Money, John Murray Learning, 2018, 263

During my agency life, we've had numerous people come to us over the years with their 'great' ideas ('eBay for dogs' was a personal highlight). While these are great ideas after you've had a few glasses of wine, the reality is that, in most cases, no one either wants or needs this idea. An idea without a business model, some perceived value, or a fair price exchange is unlikely to work, no matter how much money you throw at it.

The good news is that you can turn your idea, even something seemingly very simple, into something your ideal client wants to buy, and that's what we're going to do now.

Sell them what they want and give them what they need.

When you package up what they want and deliver what they need, people will be happy they have bought what they thought they wanted, and delighted when they find it contained what they really needed.

Here's an example from our agency.

We use WordPress to build websites for our clients, which needs regular updating and a lot of behind the scenes looking after in order to keep the website running as expected.

At first, we tried to sell this service to clients after we had made the website, by trying to explain in detail all of the behind the scenes work we were doing and why maintaining the website was so important. We really struggled to sell this service, people couldn't understand all the technical work we were telling them needed to be done. People instead opted to pay for fixes and updates when they needed them. This often meant a lot of reactive work for us fixing broken websites that had not been kept up to date, which takes longer and costs the client a lot more in the long run.

Then we had a breakthrough moment. We realised that what people wanted was for the website to be up to date and online. They didn't like the surprise costs of the website going offline or paying for content updates. We'd been selling this the wrong way around all this time. We had been selling what we wanted to sell, i.e. maintenance, not what people wanted to buy, i.e. a functioning, up to date and online website.

Nobody likes having to pay to have their car serviced, very few people take enjoyment from applying updates to their laptop or phone. But they have to happen sometime and if you delay them long enough you don't get to choose when it happens or how much it costs.

So, we made one simple change to what we were selling. We started selling what people wanted, which was to keep the website online and the content up to date. We called this service a Care Plan, rather than ongoing maintenance. We included website content updates and said that we'd take care of all the behind the scene things too. We started selling this as part of the website build, so when you buy the website you also buy the Care Plan.

After making these simple changes to how we talked about what we were selling, everyone who buys a website also buys a Care Plan. We've not changed what we're selling, we've changed how we offer it. Now it's what the clients' want (updates and peace of mind) and gives them what they need (preventive maintenance).

In this chapter we're going to be working on how you offer what you do in a way that your ideal client will want to buy.

19

The tension of change - from here to there

I bet that the products and people you recommend the most are the ones that helped you make a change in your life. It might not have been 'life-changing', it might have changed the way you take notes, exercise or organise your time. But a change happened.

Change can mean many things and is different for everyone. Without getting too deep here, what I am saying is that most of the recommendations I follow up on include a phrase similar to "It's changed the way I..."

"Working with Simon has changed the way I think about marketing."

"Using Xero has changed the way we manage the finances in our business."

"Reading 'The Soul of Money' changed the story I was telling myself about money."

I believe people are looking for change, even if they don't know it yet. People connect with change on an emotional level, and when they hear about someone else's change and it resonates with them, that is a powerful motivator for them to find out more. It creates tension.

As we have established, marketing is about creating and releasing tension. The possibility of change is one of the most effective ways to do this.

Ethical marketing is all about helping people see that change is possible, how they might make that change and supporting them with or enabling that change.

Through your marketing, you're showing them a change they might like to make. They don't have to take that path of change, they may find their own, but if you can tell them the story they've been waiting to hear, and show them how you can take them to a place they want to go, making a change they want to make, they're likely to choose to come with you.

Do I have to make change happen?

What you deliver for a client, be it a physical or digital product or a service, might not at first glance appear to make a 'change' in their lives. However, not everything can be, or needs to be, life-changing for it to be considered change. Sometimes simply making something easier or quicker can feel like a change, providing peace of mind, helping with capacity, or delivering skills that someone else doesn't have are all changes in their own way.

There are some businesses that deliver something that is simply transactional. People need the thing, they deliver the thing.

If this feels like what you do, I encourage you to take another look, as I have only come across a handful of such businesses in 20 years of working with small businesses. Almost all businesses are delivering change in some way.

No matter how small the change might feel to you, stick with it for the next exercise and see if your perception changes.

How do products make change happen?

Later in the book, we're going to look at how you can deliver products for clients at different stages: before, during and after you deliver what you do. In order to do this, we need to understand more about what change your ideal client is looking for.

When a client starts working with you they are in a certain place. This could be emotional, physical, cognitive or spiritual. Through their work with you, using your method, they will end up in a different place. Hopefully, the place they wanted to end up - even if they didn't realise it when they started. The difference between where they start and where they end is the change they seek to make.

We can only begin to deliver what they want to buy by understanding this.

Next, we will start to understand the change in more detail, from the client's perspective.

"If you're not willing to produce change, then you really have no options. Cost reduction through industrial management is your only path forward."[15]

---

[15] Seth Godin, The song of significance, Penguin Business 2023, 131

EXERCISE: Future Island

To help people understand and contextualise the change they seek and what it will be like to work with you, we create your method. This is one of the most powerful marketing tools because it helps you articulate where someone is now and where they want to be. Before we focus on the method, we need to be able to articulate these two places in the client's own words.

To illustrate this I am going to remix an idea first introduced to me by Tad Hargrave of Marketing for Hippies[16]. The idea is to visualise the change the client is seeking to make as being like travelling between two islands. They start at Present Island and they want to go to Future Island.

Some people might not yet know about Future Island. They are busy doing their own thing on Present Island. At some point, they become aware of Future Island and what it's like. Some people will want to find out if they can go there. They will look for a map and a guide. What we're going to create later is the map; and with the marketing you'll do in the last three sections of the plan, you will establish yourself as a guide for those looking to go to Future Island.

Before we create this, we need to understand what Future Island is like, and why people might want to go there.

We'll start by thinking about the situation your ideal clients find themselves in now. This is sometimes referred to as their lived experience. This is what life is like on Present Island.

---

[16] https://www.youtube.com/watch?v=hPUuUzDbW2Y

Imagine your ideal client going about their day-to-day business.

What are they...

- Thinking
- Feeling
- Doing
- Experiencing
- Avoiding
- Delaying
- Pondering
- Creating
- Worried about
- Fearful of

Note down answers to these questions where you feel you have an understanding; leave out any that don't feel right or that you don't have an understanding of.

Your understanding of your ideal client's current situation may come from lived experience, perhaps you have been where the people you work with are now. It might come from years of experience of working with these people, so you've seen these things time and time again.

If your niche is new and you're still learning about it, that's ok. In the next few conversations you have with prospective clients, you can start to observe if any of these things come up and if so in what way.

Whatever your level of understanding, try and identify which of these prompts are relevant to your ideal client and note down anything that comes to mind. Try not to overthink this, just write down the words that occur to you; we're not going to be using your answers verbatim, so for now it's just getting the ideas out of your head onto paper or screen.

Next, we need to think about where the client is likely to end up after working with you. This is where we think about Future Island and what life is like there.

Think about some clients who you've recently worked with. What words did they use to describe what they felt like, were thinking, were doing when working together came to an end?

In other words, how did they articulate the change they made after they had finished working with you?

On the same piece of paper, write down what your client might be...

· Thinking
· Feeling
· Doing
· Experiencing
· Achieving
· Practising
· Receiving
· Looking forward to
· Hopeful for
· Able to do now

Note down answers to these questions where you feel you have an understanding; leave out any that don't feel right or that you don't have an understanding of.

If you're struggling with these, or you don't have a lot of experience yet, you might like to start with the opposite of the words you wrote down for where they start from.

These prompts and your answers are not final. This is just the start of the process and I encourage you not to overthink this; just write down what comes to mind. We'll be working on these a number of times so these words can evolve, be removed or be added to.

This exercise helps you build a succinct answer to the question of what working with you is like. It also helps you to use the client's language which makes it easier to resonate and connect with them in your marketing.

20

What's stopping them

Another thing to consider is what might be stopping them from making the change they want to make or getting to the place they want to be. For some people this can be very clear and easy to describe, for others, it can be more complicated and perhaps linked to an emotional state. Even if you don't go on to talk openly in your marketing about what is stopping them, having an awareness of their current situation, or their lived experience, can add an extra level of empathy to your marketing content.

Later in the book, you will learn all about how to create content and one of the things we will draw on at this point is what your client may be thinking, feeling and doing and what's stopping them.

EXERCISE: What's stopping them?

Place yourself in their shoes. Picture them sitting at their desk, on a chair, in a field, on their bike - wherever you imagine your ideal client being when they're thinking about the things that you'd work with them on.

When you imagine them considering their current situation and where they would like to end up, ask these questions:

- What is it that is holding them back?
- What is the first step they need to take and why aren't they taking it?
- Why might they be hesitating?
- Do they have any preconceptions about the process or the destination?
- Are they lacking clarity on the pathway that lies between Present Island and Future Island?

Note down answers to these questions where you feel you have an understanding; leave out any that don't feel right or that you don't have an understanding of.

21

Your value from the client's perspective

You might know, and be able to clearly see, that a prospective client would benefit from working with you – *they* have to be able to see this as well before they can commit.

Clients won't commit to something they don't think they want or don't feel they are ready for.

This is where most people go wrong in their marketing. They jump in with all the reasons why the person needs what they're offering, they explain why working with them would be great and then ask for the sale.

With a considered purchase the client needs time to consider and decide if this work is right for them before they feel ready to commit.

To better articulate the reasons the client would benefit from working with you we need to consider their needs and wants.

Your ideal client's needs and wants are very different things. We all use a combination of these when making decisions and in the case of a purchase, in assessing the value to us.

To understand the client's point of view better it's important to understand the difference between their perceived needs and wants.

Needs

A need is something that is necessary for survival or for achieving a basic level of wellbeing. Examples of needs include food, shelter, clothing, healthcare, and safety. These are things that we must have in order to live and function in society.

Needs are often categorised according to Maslow's Hierarchy Of Needs[17]:

- **Physiological needs** – those that are vital to survival - food, water, shelter.
- **Safety needs** – health and wellness, safety against accidents and injury.
- **Social needs** – human emotional needs, feeling connected to other humans.
- **Esteem needs** – self-respect, appreciation and the desire to be respected by others.
- **Self-actualisation needs** - fulfilling of self-potential, exploitation of talents, capabilities, and potential for change.
- **Cognitive needs** - gaining knowledge and understanding.
- **Aesthetic needs** - appreciation and creative expression of beauty and form.
- **Transcendence needs** - looking beyond the physical self in search of meaning.

For the privileged of this world, their physiological and safety needs are met, so they overlook them as needs. They are able to think about needs beyond those necessary for survival.

---

[17] https://www.verywellmind.com/what-is-maslows-hierarchy-of-needs-4136760

Although not always experienced as a hierarchy, these categories help us see that needs are complex and not often the topic of casual conversation or mass media. However, they are always present within us and are more important to some than others.

Some prospective clients will be very aware of the needs that they have, others will be unaware of them. Being unaware of a need doesn't mean that it is invisible, or not felt in some way. It is often the case that the person is simply not yet able to articulate this need or frame it in a way that they understand, or to contextualise it or connect it to a behaviour.

As such, needs can be easily overlooked, unconsciously bypassed or avoided in your first interaction with a prospective client or your audience. This is the reason some clients can't see what you can see so clearly.

Wants

A want is something that is desired or preferred, it is not necessary for survival or basic wellbeing. Examples of wants include luxury items, entertainment, and leisure activities. These are things that while we might enjoy having them, we can live without.

Wants are often what a person thinks they need to address or act upon. They are most likely what a person has in mind when they seek out a solution to a perceived problem or frustration.

Once someone has decided that they *want* something, trying to persuade them that they actually *need* something different is very difficult.

This is where most marketing falls down, because most people are trying to advertise a *need* to people who have already decided that they *want* something else. It's an uphill struggle trying to persuade such people that they in fact need something different.

For your marketing to be effective it's far easier to help people understand what they might want, to offer a new perspective, or help them connect with new ideas. In this way, you invite people to form their own ideas of what they want.

Why do people choose wants?

People often make purchasing decisions based on wants over needs for several reasons:

Emotional appeals: Adverts often appeal to our emotions and desires, rather than our logical thinking. They use persuasive tactics to create a sense of urgency and convince us that we need a product, even if it's a want rather than a need.

Social pressure: People may also feel pressure from their peers or social circles to have certain products or brands. This is the fear of losing status, or the lure of gaining it. This pressure can be influenced by trends, social media, and even the desire to fit in or appear successful.

Immediate gratification: Wants often offer immediate gratification, while needs may require more time and planning to show results. People may prioritise the short-term satisfaction of a want over the long-term benefits of meeting their needs.

Lack of awareness: Some people may not be fully aware of their needs, or may not prioritise them as highly as they should. They may also lack knowledge or understanding of how their purchasing decisions impact their long-term financial and personal wellbeing.

Ineffective decision-making skills: Making informed and effective purchasing decisions requires critical thinking skills, planning, and financial literacy. People who lack these skills may be more likely to make impulsive or poorly considered purchasing decisions based on wants rather than needs.

Overall, wants and needs both play important roles in people's purchasing decisions, so it's important to recognise the difference between them and to consider how we speak about them with prospective clients in order to help them make an informed decision.

Fake needs

Sometimes people's wants can feel like needs, especially when people are bombarded with advertisements and social pressures to buy certain products and look a certain way. These are sometimes called 'fake needs' and manipulative marketers can use them to instil fear and a lack of status in order to motivate a sale.

We're going to use needs in a different way, by considering the wants a prospective client may have and how these are connected to their needs, even if unconsciously.

Most people can't articulate what they want eloquently. They want it anyway. So if you ask people what they want, they may not be able to tell you. Part of ethical marketing is to use your expertise and deeper understanding of a client's wants and underlying needs to articulate them in a way that when someone sees them, they say, "That's me."

Even if you are aware that through working with you, they might well work on and even resolve these needs, it is not always clear to them (yet). It is the wants that you can initially speak to in your marketing, knowing that in time you will work on the needs your client may have and cannot as yet articulate or understand.

At the start of the client relationship, you are the 'expert' and are likely to have a deeper understanding than they do of their underlying needs.

In considering their needs and wants, you are looking at the bigger picture, and applying your knowledge and understanding to where they are now.

"I need a productivity coach..."

Let's imagine the example of someone who is looking for a coach because they feel they need help with their productivity. They believe they need someone to help them 'get more done'.

The chances are that this person is feeling stressed and that they have too much to do. They might use words and phrases like time management, prioritisation or outsourcing to describe what they perceive the problem to be.

Their underlying needs might relate to the emotions they are feeling relating to a 'lack of control'. They may have anxiety around work-life balance. They may be feeling imposter syndrome[18] in relation to their work or a sense of dissatisfaction about what they are achieving in the world.

It is far more likely that they will talk about, or be able to articulate, their wants rather than their needs. Rightly or wrongly, it's the language they are using to try and understand and communicate their lived experience.

From the client's viewpoint what they want to be is more productive

---

[18] A psychological occurrence in which an individual doubts their skills, talents, or accomplishments and has a persistent internalised fear of being exposed as a fraud. - https://en.wikipedia.org/wiki/Impostor_syndrome

with their time. So, with our marketing we should talk with empathy to that viewpoint and help them understand more about these wants and how they might be connected.

When marketing, what we do not want to do is overcomplicate things by trying to explain the potential client's underlying need. This is not the time to try to fix the problem or to overwhelm them by explaining to them what they 'need'. Even if it is clear to you.

With a better understanding of a problem comes a deeper desire to resolve it. With an understanding of your client's needs and wants you can resist this urge to jump in and overwhelm them, instead letting them discover things at their own pace.

EXERCISE: Needs and wants

When thinking about people's needs and wants, use the following prompts:

- What questions are they asking?
- How do they describe what they want to a friend or colleague?
- What would they type into a search engine to learn more?

Think back to the productivity coach example. What would the answers be to the above questions? Perhaps these:

- They are asking how they can get more done in the day, how they can stay focused, and how they can get through their to-do list.
- They describe themselves as busy, tired, overwhelmed and in need of another coffee.
- They would search for ways to be more productive, ways to get more done.

From these answers, we can see that what they want is focus, more time, and efficiency.

What we might know, that they can't yet see, is they need: better sleep, a way of prioritising what they do, ways to say no to less important things, a long-term focus to motivate them and give direction.

If we were to talk to the client about what we can see up front they would not believe that we are able to deliver what they want. Even though it might be what they really need. So when we do our marketing, we would talk about what they want and then deliver to them through our work what they really need.

Imagine your ideal client sitting and thinking about the situation they find themselves in. Then note down your answers to these questions:

- What questions are they asking themselves?
- How do they describe what they want to a friend or colleague?
- What would they type into a search engine to learn more?
- How would you summarise what they think they *want*?
- How would you summarise what you think they *need*?

22

Creating what your ideal client wants to buy

What you know about your client, their situation, their needs and their wants are different to what the client thinks about them. Not because you can't be inside your client's head and experience their feelings directly (which you can't) but because you have what is known as 'the curse of knowledge'. Your experience and understanding of your clients is sometimes at a level beyond where the client is when they start to seek change in their lives.

The client will perceive value in what you do in many different ways. Fundamentally it comes down to them understanding your *who*, *what* and *why*. We have established what your client's likely wants and needs are, and we have some clarity on their frustrations, fears, and aspirations. We now need to communicate this to them in a way that makes it simple to understand.

We need to be able to articulate what you do in both a succinct and engaging way as well as on a more detailed and deeper level for those who really want to understand and contextualise it.

An effective way to do this is by illustrating that you understand where the client is now and where they want to be.

The prospective client may use different language to express where they are now and where they want to end up. They will typically, not always, begin by expressing their wants and they may, or may not, be able to articulate their needs.

Your marketing is an opportunity to start the work of connecting these two together. It might not happen before your work begins, but by thinking about how wants and needs relate you can ensure you're not overwhelming prospective clients by focusing on the things that they are not yet ready to talk/think about.

23

How to answer the question, "What do you do?"

What you do is not the answer to the question "What do you do?" This may seem a bit of a paradox. Surely what you do is what your clients think you do. In most cases, however, the opposite is true. Clients don't value the detail of what you do as much as they value the clarity of how you help them resolve their frustrations and deliver what they want.

With the clarity that comes from working with you, they may later see that there was much more involved and that the work itself is where the real value lies. Until they understand this, it is a waste of time, energy and everyone's brainpower to think that you have to know the details in order to see the value.

As we will see later, in most cases you don't need to communicate anything beyond 'what's in it for them' for prospective clients to see the value and feel confident about buying. Sometimes they even feel relieved or reassured that you're not trying to confuse them with science or overcomplicate the process.

So the 'what' in the question is not what you do. It's what's in it for the client. It's what they get out of working with you, it's the change they make, it's where they end up and how that feels to them. It's about them, not you.

EXERCISE: What do you do?

Although many people dislike this question, and many people cringe when asked, it's a question people want to know the answer to. Let's put aside any judgements you may have of the question, or the people who ask it, and consider how you can answer it in a creative way that gets people curious.

From what you now know about your ideal client, let's consider how you can answer this question in a way that tells them more than just your 'job title'.

Here are some examples of how you might answer the question:

- I work with clients who are (thinking/feeling/doing) things like this, and guide them through making a change so that they (think/feel/do) things like that.
- I work with clients who are (where they are now) and get them to (where they want to be).
- Have you ever (felt/thought/done) this? I work with people who do and I help them (think/feel/do) that.

Notice that none of these answers includes what you do. It's all about the client, and what's in it for them. You can be as playful or provocative as you like with your answer. Read the room and see what would get someone thinking, or the conversation moving.

84

Write down your answer to the question: What do you do?

24

WHAT BOX

In the WHAT box write down your answers to these questions using your client's language:

- What do you do?
- What is your ideal client's life like now?
- Where does that client want to go?
- What's stopping them?
- What are the client's needs and wants?

25

BOX 3: Why can they trust you to deliver it?

WHO	WHAT	WHY ★
CONNECT	CONSIDER	COMMIT

It's time to look at how you can build trust and demonstrate to your ideal client why they can believe that you will deliver on your promise.

By the end of this chapter, you will be able to answer these questions:

- Why change?
- Why now?
- Why you?

Once someone understands that they're in the right place because they recognise themselves in your *who*, they understand and contextualise the change they might like to make, the work time and energy involved and they believe your method is the right fit for them, the last thing they want to confirm is why you. They will be asking themselves what it is about you that makes you best placed to guide them in making this change.

The work here then is to communicate why you can deliver on the promise that you are going to make. One way to do this would be to simply list your qualifications, previous job roles or other relevant experience. This is unlikely to impress because lots of people may have the same pieces of paper or job descriptions. What prospective clients really want to know is what you're bringing to them that no one else can bring.

One of the best ways to do this is with a story, not the kind of story that you would tell to a child, or an adult for that matter, but one that weaves together empathy, authority and change in a way that will resonate and connect with your ideal client.

We're going to look at a number of different ways of telling your story and in later chapters will look at a number of different ways of sharing that story. Because your story is unique to you it means that when you tell your story you will stand out from everybody else because nobody else does what you do quite like you do it.

Storytelling expert Susan Payton explains in her book The Business of Stories that, *"Stories separate you from the rest of the market, showing (rather than telling) your true value and, in doing so, differentiating you from your competitors in a way they can never copy. When you do that, you're in a market of just one: you."*[19]

The word *why* carries with it quite a loaded meaning in the business world. Your BIG WHY is a common way people describe the change they seek to make in the world. Simon Sinek's best-selling book, Start With Why, places your *why* at the very centre of your business and explains how brands with a clear and powerful *why* outperform those that don't.

For many people their *why* is less grandstanding, less megaphone. In more ethical marketing your *why* is the reason your client can trust you to deliver the promise you are making. It doesn't have to be your plan to change the world.

"To decide who to buy from, your [client] will look for who they feel connected to, who makes them feel listened to, understood and important. They will choose the person, business or brand they believe will 'get' them and help them survive and thrive. Storytelling is how you help them make that connection to you."[20]

Your *why* is the story you tell to your clients. You don't have to share everything and it isn't the history of you. It doesn't have to be a 'once upon a time...' tale. Let's look at what stories you can tell.

---

[19] Susan Payton, The Business Of Stories, Rethink Press 2022, 106

[20] Susan Payton, The Business Of Stories, Rethink Press 2022, 37

26

Tell the story your ideal client has been waiting to hear

"The way we make things better is by caring enough about those we serve to imagine the story that they need to hear. We need to be generous enough to share that story so they can take action that they'll be proud of."[21]

Sometimes you will have lived the same experience as your ideal client, other times you will have observed the experience of your ideal client many times before in your work. One element of telling your story to your client is to show them that you have been down this path before, by showing them that either you or others like them have been where they are now and through working with you have got to where they wanted to be. In doing so you can demonstrate to your client you are ideally placed to guide them in making the change they seek to make. As Susan Payton explains, *"People trust clarity and consistency, so being clear about what you do, who for and why helps you tell a story that builds trust."*[22]

---

[21] Seth Godin, This Is Marketing, Penguin Business 2018, 19

[22] Susan Payton, The Business Of Stories, Rethink Press 2022, 53

Who is the hero?

In The Hero's Journey by Joseph Campbell, a character meets a guide, who gives them a plan and calls them to action, which either ends in success or failure. This story format forms the basis for many of the stories told in books and films. When telling a story, it is really easy to place yourself as the hero in the story. If you talk about how you have overcome obstacles, achieved all of the things that you wanted to achieve, made lots of money doing what you wanted to do, run a successful business, etc., etc. you are talking about *you* as the hero. It's a very common narrative, especially on social media.

People rely on heroes, people follow heroes, and people celebrate heroes. However, if they are looking to make a change in *their* lives they don't look for a hero to help them. They instead look for someone to guide them, to make *them* the hero.

If we think back to the mountain climbing analogy earlier in the book, I described standing at the bottom talking about how great it will be when you reach the top. Imagine if I had told you about all these amazing photos I had of me at the top that I had shared on my Instagram feed and how impressed they all were at my accomplishment. This is not a very enticing proposition for someone who is looking to climb the mountain themselves, the person they are looking for is someone who has a map, knows the way to the top, and is going to take a photo of *them* at the top so that they can celebrate *their* achievement. They are looking for a guide, not a hero.

Creating your stories

There are three story variations that you can use in different ways to tell different stories. In this section, we're going to look at a core theory of storytelling and then learn from a true storytelling expert how to tell your story.

The stories of self, us and now

Author Marshall Ganz created a simple way to look at the stories we tell from three perspectives. These perspectives help us to tell a complete story in different ways to people at different stages in their own journey. The three stories are:

The story of self

Is when you talk about change you have made in relation to the change your client is seeking to make. It's a chance to show that your story aligns with that of your client, that you have points of connection, similarity or shared experiences. It's not a sob story or a tale of 'woe is me'. It is not the history of you.

The story of us

Is where you show that their story truly unfolds when you work together rather than alone. It's the things from your life that speak to the place where your client is now and where they want to be. What connected those points for you, and how does this make that same connection for them?

The story of now

Is where you talk about why now is the time to start the process of change, and how you see the hurdles and obstacles stopping them. You talk about how you have been here before and you made it to the end. It's where you reassure them that you will be there for them, you have the map, your compasses are pointing in the same direction, and you invite them to take the hardest step, the first one.

Where the magic happens

So far this might all sound a bit abstract, and for a while, I struggled to wrap my head around how to actually put fingers to keyboard and write these stories. That is until I read Susan Payton's book The Business of Stories. Susan has connected together the three stories you need to tell with some very familiar words: who, what and why.

"Between your personal story and your business story lies your why: the reason you do what you do. Between your business story and your [client] story lies your value: how you help your [clients] win. And, between your personal story and your [client] story you'll find your people: the 'ideal' clients you feel passionately called to serve."[23]

(Note: in the following image, "customer story" is equivalent to "client story".)

---

[23] Susan Payton, The Business Of Stories, Rethink Press 2022, 17

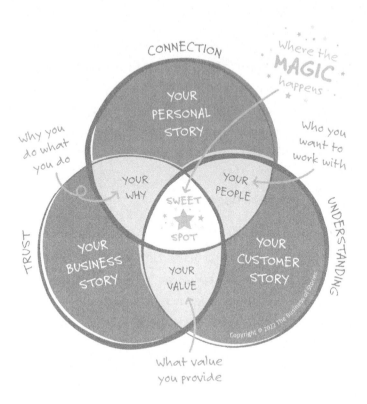

24

In this section I am going to share a brief interpretation of these three stories so you can have a go at writing your own.

24 Susan Payton, The Business Of Stories, Rethink Press 2022, 17

27

Your personal story - the story of self - why you?

This is not your life story. It is the highlights of that story that explain who you are and how you got to be where you are now. It is where you share the overlaps, similarities or connections that you believe exist in both your story and that of your ideal client. Its aim is to enable your ideal client to see some of themselves, their feelings, thoughts or actions in your story.

If you're a little unsure about sharing, Susan says, *"Being vulnerable and sharing the good and bad helps others to feel encouraged about their journey and find the strength to get back up, dust themselves off and carry on. Just like you did."*[25]

Here's a fun way to get started, open the audio recorder app on your phone, press record and then try to tell your life story in two minutes. Then listen back to it and see what stands out for you (other than the sound of your own voice). From this, you can start to expand on the

---

[25] Susan Payton, The Business Of Stories, Rethink Press 2022, 51

points that you believe will resonate and cut out those that don't need to be in there. If you have lived experience of the change they seek to make then share how you were before, what you did to change, and how you were afterwards.

Here are some words of wisdom from Susan to help add a bit more magic to your story:

"Share the story of what led you here, doing what you now do. Why did you choose to do this work? How did you find your 'thing'? Why does the work you do matter? Do people know how much it means to you? Why do you care? Does your audience understand who you love working with and why, and what a great result you can help them get?"[26]

This story is a great way to get people curious. It helps people who are unaware make that first connection to the opportunity for change.

You can use this story on your website, social or in podcast interviews. Keep it concise and to the point. You can write your memoirs another time.

---

[26] Susan Payton, The Business Of Stories, Rethink Press 2022, 50

28

Your business story - the story of us - why change?

This is where you tell the story of how your lived experience or experience from working with clients has taken you through the process that the client is about to start. It's where you can share the thoughts, feelings, and actions that you have seen before and then link these to what they are like after working through your process. You're not being prescriptive or trying to project the outcome, rather sharing how others like them have experienced this before. You're creating a story that explains how your method connects to where the client is now and where they want to be.

Susan explains that, *"Your [client] story starts with understanding what they're struggling with right now and what story they're telling themselves about what they can and can't do."*[27]

It's voice note time again. This time open the app, press record, and answer these questions:

---

[27] Susan Payton, The Business Of Stories, Rethink Press 2022, 64

- How did you come to be working with your last client?
- What was it like for them before you worked together?
- What did you work on with them?
- What was it like for them after you worked with them?

This is a great way to talk about your work without directly talking about it.

You can edit your answers into an answer to the question "what do you do?" or "how does working with you work?"

Sharing this story can help people refer people to you, and help those who are feeling curious become inspired to learn more. It confirms what people think they know or understand about what they have learned so far and helps them make a decision about if the change you are describing is right for them.

You can use it at networking events, in conversations, during interviews, and on your website.

29

Your client story - the story of now - why now?

This story is where you create some helpful tension and give confidence to those who are inspired to help them feel motivated to take the first step. You explain how you can support and guide them, and that you see, hear and understand where they are now and what lies ahead.

Here's how Susan describes this story:

"For people to act, there must be something at stake. Otherwise, they won't be motivated enough to put in the effort to do what needs to be done. Unpacking your [client] story helps you identify if they're likely to be looking for help before the problem grows, or after it has shown up ... Talking about the consequences you can help your [client] avoid, even if those consequences are that nothing changes, needs to be a part of the story you're telling."[28]

---

[28] Susan Payton, The Business Of Stories, Rethink Press 2022, 69

It might be helpful to think of the feeling like the end of a TED talk, the conclusion of a pitch or if both of those are out of your comfort zone, the last paragraph of a good novel that leaves you wanting more.

Let's get the voice note app out one last time. This time press record and imagine you're sitting opposite a client who is ready to make a change yet they're not quite sure if they should begin. Imagine they're putting it off because they're nervous.

- What would you say to them to help them feel reassured, to understand more about what lies ahead and what they can expect?
- What story can you share with them about someone (maybe you) who has been there before?

This is a great story to share when you are asking people to take the first step. It can give people the confidence they need to make the commitment to book a call or get in touch. This is often a big step as it is unknown and self-motivated, so any confidence you can inspire here can really help those who feel drawn to make the change.

You can also use this story during calls with prospective clients and on your website.

EXERCISE: Write your stories

Using the three story sections write out your three short stories: your personal story, your business story, and your client story.

These three stories will not be perfect the first time and they will likely evolve and change over time as you deepen your understanding of your clients and your work. That's ok, you can revisit this as many times as you need to. The important thing is to get something written down.

After all, *"Well begun is half done,"* is the timeless wisdom of Mary Poppins!

The three stories to write are:

- Your personal story – the story of self – why you?
- Your business story – the story of us – why change?
- Your client story – the story of now – why now?

We'll leave off this section with some words of motivation from Susan.

"Sharing stories is a powerful way to demonstrate the true value of what you help people do. The more compelling your stories of success, the more people will understand what it is you're ultimately helping them achieve and the more valuable they will perceive your product or service to be."[29]

If you want more detailed guidance on writing your stories then I highly recommend you invest in Susan's book, The Business of Stories, which will guide you step by step through the whole process.

---

[29] Susan Payton, The Business Of Stories, Rethink Press 2022, 105

30

WHY BOX

In the WHY box write down your answers to these questions - if they don't fit, summarise them in one sentence or with some keywords to remind you at a glance, and then use other sheets/pages for the longer versions.

Remember, this plan is just a reminder - it should be a useful prompt for you about what each story is about.

- Why change?
- Why now?
- Why you?

IV

Value - Product - Price

31

Communicating your value

Before we carry on with our 6-box plan, there are three things we need to work on that will make the rest of the boxes much easier to complete and will make your final plan a lot clearer. These are method, product and price. In this chapter, we'll deal with method.

Now that you understand who your ideal client is and what they want and need, it's time to think about how you will deliver or guide them to the outcome, feeling or insight they're looking for. We do this by using your method.

Your method is *not* your product. Your method is a description of the change that the client will experience.

In a practical sense, it is *what* you do in your work, and will most likely be a process or flow that you follow, based on a mixture of training, experience, research, your values and your story. By blending this all together into a method, you create a way of articulating at a high level how the client will make the change they seek to make.

Your method is unique to you, and even if someone else does the same thing, they will not have your unique way of doing it.

As Susan Payton says, *"You don't have to compete with anyone, just focus on doing what you do the way only you do it."*[30]

- Some people will be using a 'standardised' or 'licensed' process. In this case, the method is how *you* deliver that process.
- Some people will have an emergent process, within which some key concepts, ideas, starting prompts, or questions are contained.
- Some people will have a flow process with a series of waypoints that you'll pass with a client as the work unfolds.

You may have a magical blend of them all, with some of your own ideas mixed in.

Whatever method you use - it's *your* unique method.

It's likely that you spent some time developing, learning, training, and even qualifying in your method - so to expect your client to try and understand it in detail might be a tall order.

Instead, what we're looking to describe to them is a simple, easy-to-follow series of steps that they can readily understand and connect with. It illustrates to them how they can make the change they seek to make and reach the outcome, feeling or insight that they want - or need - to get to.

Put simply, your method is how you describe to someone what they will experience in getting from where they are to where they want to be - the change they seek to make. It enables them to visualise and contextualise it, so they can make an informed decision about whether they feel they are ready to commit to the work or not.

---

[30] Susan Payton, The Business Of Stories, Rethink Press 2022, 109

It's about how you describe to someone who is seeking change, and beginning to look for a solution, what a good solution might be for them - without it feeling like selling. When you set out your method as a possible solution, rather than a product, it helps them 'piece together' or 'map out' in their mind how they could get where they want to go.

If they are ready, you can offer to guide them to where they want to go, and that offer is your product. We'll get to that in the next chapter.

Separating your method from your product means you can talk about your method in many different situations without it feeling like selling. This means you can write and talk about it in your content, and share the ideas, concepts and steps of this method all without it feeling like you're trying to make a sale.

By sharing your method you're inviting someone to consider the change, the outcome, feeling or insight they are wanting to get to. You're letting them make an informed decision about the work and the commitment they will need to make to it. You're not asking them to consider investments, or time scales, so this means they can truly decide if this is right for them before they consider your offer of guidance.

Some people will consider your method and think, "That's not for me," or, "I'm not ready for that." This is a good thing, because they're not yet ready to commit (yet), so to try and persuade them otherwise is hard work, and not very ethical. These people might just need a bit more time, they might need to engage with more of your content, or simply think a little more before they feel ready.

Sharing your method openly enables them to consider the change they seek to make and the work involved in their own time at their own pace. The results of this are that the clients you end up working with are ready to start the work of making the change and want to embrace what will unfold.

32

Mapping your method

The client doesn't necessarily need to understand your method in detail or every tiny step along the way. In the earlier stages of marketing, your method is a simple way of explaining the change they are considering. You will get to the detail and a deeper level of understanding later on in your work.

One of the most effective ways to explain your method is to illustrate it in some way. You might be able to articulate a linear path, from A to B. Or perhaps it is an upwards spiral that you traverse, with each loop gaining you more understanding and insight. It might be a series of paths that a potential client can choose to take.

Think back to the Future Island exercise. When you look at the line, you can see the rough path you would take to get between the two islands. Let's imagine the client wants to take a rowing boat to Future Island.

They have two choices: they can try and understand why the route is plotted this way and where every rock and shallow was along the route.

Or they can look for a guide who knows the route and can help them row themselves to Future Island. You could try and explain all the details to them before you set off, but it's far easier to show them along the way.

However you visualise or explain it, the method should illustrate the path you guide them along from their viewpoint, not yours. The aim is to show the prospective client how they will experience working with you. We need to show them how they will get from their current situation to the place they want/need to be.

EXERCISE: Drawing your method

In this exercise, we're going to try drawing your method. In doing so, we're going to illustrate the steps or stages that a client can expect to work through. It doesn't have to include all the details of your work.

The simpler the better.

Using your notes from earlier in the book, start with where the prospective client is now, then either explain the next steps until you get to where they want to end up, or if you're still working on your method, write down the start and the end and then work out the waypoints along the way at which the client will experience progress or a change.

Here are a few examples:

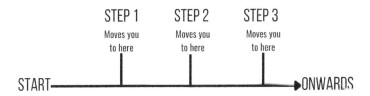

You start at the beginning like this - feeling, thinking or experiencing this

- Step 1 moves you to here
- Step 2 moves you to here
- Step 3 is where you feel, think or experience something that will feel better than where you are now.

Sometimes you might start with the client's feelings and point to your work in the middle and how that works.

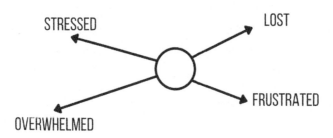

Other times you might swap it around so your work is in the middle and where they end up is at the end of the path.

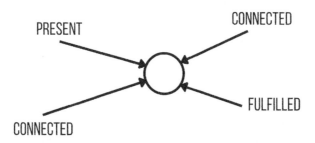

Or perhaps it might be an illustration of something that helps you visualise or explain it. How about making a cake, with your ingredients going in and different cakes coming out each time.

Or Lego bricks building something different each session.

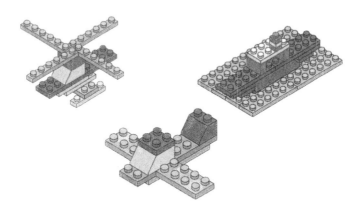

Or a series of mountains linked by bridges or cable cars to help show the process.

Draw your method, try just sketching out what it looks like to you, and see what comes out.

Try to capture some of the waypoints and key ideas/concepts that your work encompasses.

Once you have drawn something, then carry on.

Think about the outcome, feeling or insight that you guide people to and ask yourself, does the drawing illustrate that?

From your client's perspective ask:

- What do I have to do to get where I want to go?
- How will I know if it is working?
- What are some of the things I may think/feel/do along the way?
- Is there an end? Is the end a new beginning? Is this a loop?

Explaining your method

Once you've drawn your method, even if not the final version of it, the next task is to start the process of explaining it and we do this in the Consider chapter. For now, we're going to look at the next foundation: your product.

33

Creating your product

Having established or clarified your method, it's time to think about how you package that into a product you're inviting them to buy.

"It's easier to make products and services for the [clients] you seek to serve than it is to find [clients] for your products and services."[31]

Once someone has considered your method and feels they have an understanding of what's involved and the work they will need to do, or enough of an understanding to be confident that it is what they are looking for, they will naturally progress to wanting to 'do the work'. They will be looking to either work through the method on their own or for someone to guide them. This is where your product comes in.

Before we carry on, let's clarify what I mean when I say product, as some of you might be thinking, "I don't sell a product, I deliver a service."

---

[31] Seth Godin, This Is Marketing, Penguin Business 2018, 6

In a broad sense, what you deliver may typically be thought of as a service, like accountancy, coaching or consulting. But when a client thinks of these broad terms it can feel vague when considering what they want from that service.

They might wonder, "How much consulting do I need?"

In his book Entrepreneur Revolution, Daniel Priestley, describes a product as, "...a consistent way to deliver an outcome that the client wants."[32] With this in mind it becomes clearer to think of the way you deliver your work as a product rather than as a service.

Your product will clearly and concisely articulate the promise that you are making to the client. It helps your client understand and contextualise what it is you are going to be doing with them and what is expected from them. It also clearly sets out the outcomes, feelings or insights that you guide people to. It may be a single product or a collection of products for those with different levels of commitment.

Commitment levels

People with an understanding of your method will naturally have different levels of commitment to it.

Some will feel no commitment at all, deciding it isn't for them. That's ok, you've saved both them and you a lot of time and energy.

Others will resonate with your method while having constraints on their time, energy, or finances. Some may have lots of one and not as much of the other. For example, someone may have a lot of money and

---

[32] Daniel Priestley, Entrepreneur Revolution, Capstone 2018, 162

not much time, and conversely, someone may have a lot of time and not much money.

When designing your product we need to consider which of these commitment levels to focus on. There is no one product that can satisfy them all.

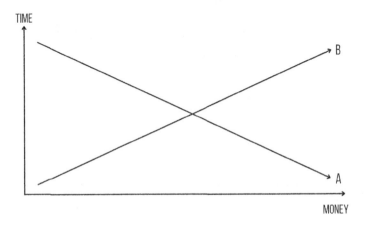

In this graph the vertical axis represents the time a prospective client has available. On the horizontal axis we have the money that they can draw on.

Line A shows someone with more time and less money, and Line B shows someone with less time and more money.

Lines A and B also show how much time *you* need to commit to delivering the method and how much you can charge in relation to the value of spending time with you.

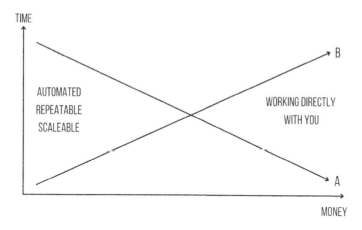

These two lines represent two different types of client, you cannot serve both of them with the same product.

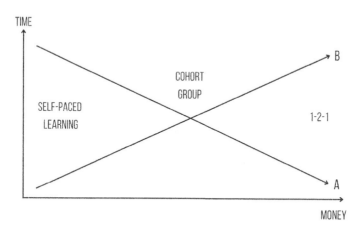

For someone with a lot of time and not much money a product that is automated in its sale and delivery works well. You might like to consider a self-paced learning programme or video course, as this fits well for clients with less money who have time that they can commit. Products that you create for this commitment level are designed to be easily repeatable and scalable and require the person with high time availability to commit their time to working through the method at their own pace. For many, this is their preferred learning style, so it should not be viewed as being less valuable, rather that it can be priced lower because you do not have to commit as much time to its delivery.

In the middle of the graph, there is a balance between time and money commitments. Here a product like a cohort-based learning programme, group work or perhaps an outcome-orientated community is a more time-effective way to deliver your value balanced with financial commitment.

For those who have more money and less time to commit to working with you, 1-2-1 work may be the best product for them. As this involves the most amount of your time, it is priced the highest out of all the products.

A product is most effective when it is supported by other products for the other commitment levels, that is to say if you make one product for each of the commitment levels you will be able to cater for prospective clients at each level.

However, I don't recommend that you try and build all of these products at the same time. It is best to work out which of these products energises you most and which one you feel you could deliver most effectively for the kind of clients that you're looking to attract. Wherever you start, you can always create a product for the other commitment levels as you progress.

Now, choose *one* product you want to work on and focus only on that as you work through the next exercise. Then, once you feel you have got this product up and running, you can revisit this chapter and work through the same exercise for the next product.

Things to consider:

- The 1-2-1 sessions option is the simplest product to create, the fastest to launch, and is often the best place to start.
- A cohort-based learning programme or community requires an established audience to launch successfully, and often requires some testimonials from people who have worked with you in the past to build trust.
- A self-paced learning course takes a lot of time to create and can be hard to sell if you have limited previous experience or track record. It is also hard to sell without a large established audience.

Once you've decided on which product you want to build, let's carry on with the exercise.

34

Creating the perfect fit

Creating a product that feels like the perfect fit is where your method comes in. You design a product that guides your ideal client through your method. Your method enables the client to make an informed decision about the work involved, by visualising and contextualising the process, making them feel more confident, comfortable, and perhaps excited about working with you.

By the time they see your offer, they will likely have read/watched your explanation of your method. It is likely that this now forms their idea of what the solution they are searching for looks and feels like. If they feel inspired or motivated to use your method to get them where they want to be they will most likely look for a guide to help them. When they do so they will be looking for someone that can guide them through your method, this will naturally bring them to your product offer. At this point, you can offer them your product which, if it maps to your method, will look and feel like the perfect fit for those who understand it and have decided that this method is what they're ready to commit to.

This way of designing your product also helps you create something that is both manageable and achievable for them. People often hesitate if something looks like too much work, will take too long, or they can't see an 'ending'. Using your method to help them contextualise the work involved helps them feel more comfortable that this is what they're looking for in terms of both timescales and workload.

The key to making your product is: **Keep It Simple**.

To create a profound product for your clients, you don't need to reinvent the wheel. You can make your life easy by using existing tools and structures that work for you, which help you to design a product that supports the lifestyle you want and reduces the pressure on you to deliver something that is beyond your capacity.

When designing your product, it is easy to get drawn into the *myth of more*. What you deliver or offer to the client doesn't have to be bigger or better or include more than anyone else.

Your product needs to be designed for your ideal client, not to compete or replicate what someone else is offering. There are two mistakes a lot of people make when designing a product:

- They try to pack it full of features and options to match or compete with everyone else in the market.
- They try to solve all of the client's problems, change all of their feelings, or inspire all of their insights.

This leads to a product that is complicated to explain and often too much to deliver. It is the main reason why 'selling' the product can feel awkward.

If your product is just full of things to bulk it out then explaining why they're all in there can make the conversation uncomfortable.

So, although you might feel like you need to add more to keep up, or to justify the price you want to charge, we must resist this urge and focus on what matters most: making your product feel like it is the perfect fit for what they're looking to buy.

It can also be tempting when you look at other people and see their ecosystem of products to want to emulate what they're doing. However, they most likely have spent years developing their products, and to try and create your own version in one go is unrealistic.

When you first start out, your product might simply be a series of 1-2-1 sessions. These sessions will most likely map your method.

Let's look at an example of a coaching product.

Coach Jill has a five-step method to help people become less stressed, sleep better and feel more in control of their time. She has created many blog posts, web pages and a 20-page guide all about this method and how it works.

When a client decides they want to work with Jill, she offers 1-2-1 sessions priced at £100 per session. All the client needs to do is book a discovery call.

On the face of it, this is a logical offer to make. However, how does a potential client connect the five-step method to Jill's offer of a 1-2-1 session? In short, they can't. So they are left questioning how many sessions they need? How long does the process take? Is £100 per session good value? Will it work?

Will Jill get many people booking discovery calls? The answer to confusion is always no. So, what would be a better offer? Here is an example of what could work for Jill.

Less stress - more sleep. Using my five-step method, I will work

1-2-1 with you as we reduce your stress, improve your sleep, and empower you to feel more in control of your time. There are five sessions over five weeks, priced at £500. To discuss if this process is right for you, book a discovery call with me.

This offer requires the same investment as the 1-2-1 session offer we saw before, and this one answers a lot of the potential client's questions.

The question of value is removed because the client is now considering the whole process, they're not trying to work out if they think they need five sessions or comparing Jill's hourly rate to someone else's. Packaging up your sessions and resources into a product makes them easier to understand and consider.

Myth-busting!

Some people say to me, "I work with my clients on an ongoing basis, so I can't make a product." The good news is that this process of creating a product does not prohibit that. If anything it makes it easier. It gives the client something they can contextualise and understand and commit to, making that first step easier. After delivering a product, you will know if ongoing work is the right fit for them, and you can have a different ongoing product that you offer to them, or just move to rolling sessions if that works best for you.

EXERCISE: Creating your product

Thinking about your method, what is the most effective way you can deliver the outcome, feeling or insight you guide your clients to?

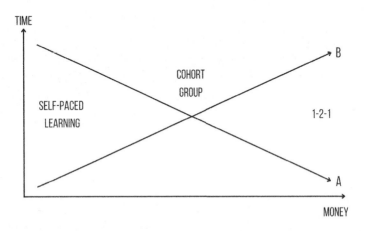

Here are some examples of products that I see often:

- A set of 1-2-1 sessions for coaching or mentoring
- A group programme
- A cohort-based learning programme
- An outcome-oriented community
- A self-paced learning course
- A book

You don't have to use all of these, or any of them if you have your own product idea. The key is that your product is seen as the perfect fit for someone who is looking for someone to guide them through your method. It's your product, so you can decide what to include.

The following four sections will offer some guidance depending on where you're at with your product offering, so skip ahead to the section that describes you if you wish. Write down your ideas and notes for the section that applies to you.

We will build on these notes later on and make a fuller description and web page. So for now just record your ideas.

I'm just starting out

If you're just starting out then it's worth looking at the commitment diagram again and thinking which of these commitment levels energises you the most, and where *your* commitment in time and energy lies.

For example, creating a self-paced learning course takes a lot of time, and because of its lower price point will take longer to generate revenue, so starting with this may not be the best choice. Conversely, creating a 1-2-1 product is relatively simple and is quick to launch. When creating a 1-2-1 product, sometimes the best place to start is simply mapping the sessions to your method.

For example, if you have six steps or waypoints in your method then you could offer six sessions, one to work on each step. If you think you need two sessions per method step, then that's ok too. Think through a few options and see what you think is the simplest to understand from the client's perspective.

If you do not have an audience already then starting with 1-2-1 can be a really good place because as you work with more people you will learn more about them and their needs and wants. You can then use this knowledge to build a group or cohort-based learning programme. As your audience grows you can offer it to those who are not yet ready to work with you on a 1-2-1 basis.

Then once you have delivered this cohort-based learning programme a few times, you can turn this material into a video or self-paced learning course for those who are not yet ready to commit to the group programme.

If you already have a large audience, offering 1-2-1 may not be the most effective because you may well find yourself being oversubscribed very quickly. In which case, it may be better to offer either self-paced learning or a cohort-based learning programme as well as a 1-2-1 option.

I already have a product

If you already have a product that you want to evolve, then look at what you deliver and how that maps to your method.

Questions to ask yourself when reviewing your product are.

- Could I create resources for clients to use before the first session or in between sessions?
- Could I deliver what the client wants in another way? How would this serve the client? How would this serve me?
- Could I create resources, worksheets, videos, prompt cards or something else useful for the client to have access to after they have finished working with me?
- How can I make their experience working with me more fluid, enjoyable, and inspirational?

I'm fully booked

If you are fully booked then creating a self-paced learning course may be a great way to add an extra stream of revenue, and free up some time. It can release time and energy you spend covering the essentials of your work that can then be focused on deeper work with your clients.

You might also like to run a group programme or cohort-based learning programme. This can be a time effective way of working with more clients without it taking more of your time to deliver.

I want to take my product to the next level

Sometimes it can be hard to think of something that feels a bit different, something that you can get excited about and feel passionate about delivering.

If this is you, then here is a thought experiment.

You can fly from London to Sydney for around £5300 business class, and £530 standard fare. Do you get 10 times more space, does it get you there 10 times faster? No, you get free food and drink, you skip the line for security, you get to wait in a nicer lounge, and your seat lies flat. Is that worth 10 times more? Some people think so.

The price people are willing to pay is based mainly on the story people tell themselves about the value they will receive.

By changing the story you tell about your product, you can change the way people perceive the value they will receive. This is particularly useful when what you're offering is not always tangible or familiar to people before they do the work.

To look at this in a different way, let's consider this question.

If you had to charge 10 times what you do now...

- How would you change what you do?
- How would you change the story you're telling?
- What would your client pay 10 times more for?

This isn't about selling more, or bumping up your price, it's an exercise designed to remove the cost element from your thinking. By allowing yourself to consider what you'd do if money was not a limiting factor you can get really creative. After all, if people are willing to pay 10 times more, what else could you do, or how would you do what you do differently?

Hint: this doesn't mean doing what you do now but harder or longer. It's about thinking about what your client really wants and reflecting on how well the story you're telling matches this.

From your thinking in this exercise is there something you can bring to your work? Even if you have to change what you charge for it, would people pay more for it?

35

Putting a price on it

In this chapter, we're going to be talking about pricing - which means we're going to have to talk about the sometimes awkward topic of money. This might feel uncomfortable before it feels comfortable, so stick with me as we're going to be covering the money and pricing topic from a few angles.

The amount of time you have to make money is limited, so pricing is really important. This is not about getting rich, rather about how to earn enough to have time and money to live the life you want to live.

I'm not going to tell you how much to charge. Instead, I'm going to look at how you can go about charging for your work and your products in a way that helps you earn what you need to earn, avoid burnout, and allow you to develop and grow your business, and yourself.

When you decide on a price for your product, you're unlikely to get it right the first time, and it can take time to settle on a price that feels right to both you and your clients.

You might be the kind of person that doesn't like to talk about money until you're having a conversation with someone who may become a client, or you might like to show your prices on your website.

You may have a product that can be purchased in different ways by individuals and companies, for which you may have different ways of pricing.

You might be just starting out, where the experience of working with clients is as valuable as any money you make.

Wherever you are, this chapter is designed to help you get more comfortable talking about money, by getting clear about your perceived value.

36

Your story about money

Everyone has a different relationship with money, often based on the story we tell ourselves about it. This story will in some way be influenced by your previous experiences with money.

It will also be influenced by conversations you have with peers, clients, suppliers and service providers, and perceptions you have of yourself and others.

Perhaps without being aware of it, your upbringing and parents' relationship to money has influenced how you feel about spending, saving and risk-taking. Your exposure to people who were perceived as rich or poor will have set your internal scale for how this is defined and publicly judged.

Where you have travelled, the work you have done and the jobs you have held all contribute to the story you tell yourself and others about money.

Either unconsciously, or consciously, we invariably associate our self-worth with money. It also influences our internal measure of status and shame.

As with much of life, we can choose the story we tell ourselves about money and use this to inform the choices we make in our business and about pricing.

If you look at your prices and think it feels expensive then ask yourself – What story am I telling myself where this feels expensive? What am I comparing this to?

Getting comfortable with charging

Let's set out a clear definition of money so we can see that we're talking about the same thing.

"The purpose of money is to create an efficient, fair and universal exchange of value to serve the growth of humanity. It is used to cope with an uncertain future, trusting that you can store value today for a purchase tomorrow or further into the future."[33]

Money is the most common exchange we make for goods and services and so that's what we're going to be talking about here. It doesn't have to be limited to money if something else would serve you, like a skill swap or a trade of time, resources or services.

Pricing is the balance of fair value with fair price. When these two balance there is a fair exchange. Put another way, price is what you say people will get, value is what they feel like they received.

Value then is what you work with your clients on, as perceived by them. Value is all in the mind and people value different things. Some value

---

[33] Rob Moore, Money, John Murray Learning 2018, 61

utility over appearance and have little regard for the status of what they buy. Others value appearance and the perceived status it implies with their peers over utility; which explains the world of designer or luxury goods.

You cannot control the value that a person attaches to your work. You can signal and position in a way that indicates how you would like it to be perceived.

If you deliver on your promise then clients receive fair value, and in doing so they might desire to receive more and perhaps refer you to others to share the value.

In a fair exchange, you have offered a product that a client perceives as valuable enough to pay for. When you receive fair financial compensation, this also buys you time. It means you can afford to only work when you said you would work, pause and reflect, re-energise and commit time to self-development.

"When you are the cheapest you're not promising change. You're promising the same but cheaper."[34]

In an unbalanced transaction where you do not receive fair compensation for your value, you are at risk of creating a draining spiral of time and energy. Money stories such as guilt, lack of confidence, social beliefs or emotions can get in the way of pricing and make it hard to fairly price your value. When you have to work longer, you eat into the time you need to look after yourself and your clients.

The other side of this imbalance is if you charge too high a price in comparison to the value you deliver. In this case, it can be perceived as

---

[34] Seth Godin, This Is Marketing, Penguin Business 2018, 182

unfair, greedy or worse still as ripping people off. You may be able to temporarily boost sales by overpromising with a big claim. This will bounce back on you once the reality of the lack of value is received.

When you're able to make a fair exchange, it means you can make a fair profit. This profit might be in the form of more money or more time. This can be spent on developing yourself, your business or building the life you want. It is important to recognise that you need to, and are expected to, make a fair profit in running your business, and it is essential if you want to avoid burnout and continue to serve your clients with energy and enthusiasm.

So, now we understand the exchange that is happening – fair value at a fair price – we need to work out how your value will be priced.

Pricing is a point of view

Some people resist setting or choosing their own price. They feel that there is a price limit in their sector, niche or social group that can't be exceeded. Or they feel that what they deliver is 'standardised', and that prices are controlled. If your product is designed in such a way that it looks and feels the same as everybody else in the market then it's easy to compare to everybody else in the market.

This is why basing your product on your method is a really great way of standing out in the marketplace. In this way, people aren't comparing like for like, which means you can set your own price which is a fair exchange.

Pricing your product is simple as long as you consider it from the buyer's point of view. The cost to you of making or delivering something is largely irrelevant because what the client is paying attention to is value. Your clients don't care as much as you do what it took for you to make something, they care about what it does for them.

Cheaper

The problem with being cheaper is that it's a race to the bottom, and as Seth Godin says.

"The problem with the race to the bottom is that you might win."[35]

Cheapness isn't the reason people buy things. There are thousands of things you could go and buy right now for less than £1. You don't because you don't want them. If being cheap was the only reason we bought things we'd all have a lot of things.

If you only show up when someone has already decided what they want and are ready to buy, then to get them to choose you, you'll have to be cheaper. You can't rely on being better, because for them to see you as better requires them to change what they want. People don't like doing this, so it's not worth showing up when people have already reached this stage in their decision making.

What you're doing by working though this book is showing up earlier in that decision making process and showing people the value you offer so you can attach a fair price to it.

Think back to the needs and wants of your ideal client. I'll wager cheapest wasn't on your list of wants, or needs. People only want cheaper when it's a tie between two things that look the same.

If people want to make a change in their lives, to turn their business around or to build their confidence then the price is not what they

---

[35] This is another phrase that Seth often says on his podcasts, but it isn't found in his books.

consider first. Before they get to that they are thinking about *who*, *what* and *why*. If they trust you to deliver on your promise then the price isn't much of a consideration.

Balancing price and value

Every purchase is a choice with one of three outcomes, the buyer can:

1. Buy what you're selling.
2. Choose to do nothing.
3. Buy something else instead.

If your product meets their perception of fair value and price, then they are likely to say yes and buy what you are selling.

If your product doesn't meet their expectation of value and/or price, they have two options – do nothing or do something else.

When the price is perceived to be high, or even too low, people will often choose to do nothing as they can't make the exchange balance for them.

If there are easy and obvious substitutes to what you sell, and their perception of your value is not met, they are likely to buy something else instead.

Part of the work of designing your product and marketing it, is to help people understand that there is no good substitute and that your product aligns with their perception of value.

Pricing is linked to value and this is linked to how you perceive and present that value. Your value lies in your method.

Here is a story to illustrate.

> *A person has a squeaky floorboard and they've tried everything to stop it squeaking, nothing has worked and it's driving them mad.*
>
> *They call a carpenter who comes over, walks on the board, hears the squeak and says it will be £60 to fix the floorboard.*
>
> *The client agrees*
>
> *The carpenter gets a wooden wedge out, taps it into a gap, sands it down so you can't even notice it. They stop the squeak in two minutes.*
>
> *"That'll be £60 please."*
>
> *"Why is that £60, it only took two minutes," the client asks?*
>
> *The carpenter replies, "It's £10 for the hammer and the wedge, and £50 for the years it took me to learn how to do the job in only two minutes."*

The value to the client is in stopping the squeak, not the time it took. Once the value is refocused on the outcome rather than the time taken, the question of value is balanced.

Once the client sees the value in your method, it's not as important to them how much each session costs or what the price breakdown is. If they perceive the value in what you are promising, they will be ready to exchange money at a fair price for you to guide them through that method using your product.

37

What are you pricing for?

When you are just starting out, you may well be pricing to attract your first clients. You may still be exploring your value and you may feel you can't easily put a price on what you deliver. This is ok and is part of the process. Very few people get the price right the first time.

There's a school of thought that says you should always charge more because you're worth it, and in the early days of your business, this can feel difficult to do. Also, you may not be charging the most you can charge when you first start out as you may be trying to attract clients. You may be pricing lower intentionally to get experience, feedback, testimonials or referrals. In the early stages, you have to be open to being flexible with your pricing.

This also applies if you already have clients and are developing a new product, course or community.

Your price is just for now, and you are allowed to change your prices.

It may be that for the niche you currently have, a certain price feels appropriate. This may change over time as you get more clients, add more to your product or move into a different or more refined niche. At this point you may choose to, and are allowed to, change your prices.

So, how can we start to work out our fair value and fair price? The fair value you have already worked on in your product, so now we need to find the fair price.

EXERCISE: What's a fair exchange?

This is a simple question of: what is the value you are exchanging worth to the client?

For example, if your career coaching often earns your client a £15,000 salary increase, then the exchange is worth anything up to that amount, or perhaps even more, considering the longer-term benefits.

For many people, the benefit they receive does not necessarily have a tangible or quantifiable outcome in a monetary sense, so it can be hard to put an exact figure against it.

Instead, think about the perceived value to the client, it might be monetary, it might be a feeling or emotion. Write down your answers to these questions:

- What would be the cost of doing nothing? Is there a cost or downside to simply not doing anything?
- What is the cost of doing something else? (e.g. working with someone else or taking a course)
- Will working with you save them time, money or energy?

Looking at your answers to these prompts. What feels like a fair price?

In this exercise, you're thinking about what the exchange is worth from the client's point of view. Not in relation to how long it takes you to deliver, or how long it took you to make it. Looking at all the different ways your product can be perceived as valuable, what price do you feel would be a fair exchange?

Acknowledgement: The challenge with setting your price is finding the point where your value balances with their perception of a fair price, resulting in a fair exchange. This takes time and many conversations with clients before it feels right. If you're not sure about your price then try it out in your next conversation and see how it goes. If they think it's too high then ask them what they're comparing it to, or why they feel like it's high.

It's not always useful to ask clients what they are willing to pay without offering some kind of guide because most people are not able to accurately set a value on intangible goods on the spot. If you're struggling to decide on a price it's unlikely your client will arrive at the perfect price in one guess.

How many clients do you need?

Once you have settled on your price (for now), you can work out how many clients you need. This might be the number of 1-2-1 clients you want to work with each month. Or it might be a blend of 1-2-1 sessions and group work. It might also include a portion from course/programme sales.

You might like to have different rates for clients, which may also include pro bono clients. The blend of sessions and prices you have is up to you, and there is no right or wrong way to it.

You can make these calculations as simple or as complex as you like. The idea is that you have an indicator of how near or far you are from where you would ideally need to be. Some months, you might not be quite there, others you may be above it. Going through this process means you can see where you are and where you want to be and make adjustments accordingly.

It's not a hard and fast rule. You don't have to charge the same for every client. What it does do is give you a number to compare against, aim for, or use as a baseline.

After 20 years of running a business, the only thing I can share from my experience is that even the best plans change fast in the real world. So hold these numbers lightly.

V

Connect - Consider - Commit

38

BOX 4: Creating the first step

WHO	WHAT	WHY
CONNECT	**CONSIDER**	★ **COMMIT**

Back to the plan! The next three boxes - Connect, Consider and Commit - we work through backwards. This gives clarity from the start on where to direct people as they go on their journey towards becoming a client.

Let's remind ourselves of that journey by thinking back to the cascade of clients. The client moves through four stages: Unaware, Curious, Inspired and Motivated. As they move through this journey we need to have somewhere to point them so they can progress their journey. If we start where they start then we have nowhere to point them. So we start at the last stage and work backwards creating the journey for them to follow.

With this in mind, we start at the end with the first step we want them to take - where they commit.

In this chapter you will work on:

· Your promise
· Your first step
· Your *why* prompts

We'll bring these three together by creating your *who*, *what*, and promise sentence.

Then you'll learn how to ensure your website has all this information on it, or create one that does.

39

Your promise

When building trust, an important thing to set out is the promise that you are making to your clients. Once someone has considered your method, and decided it's the right fit for them, they're ready to commit. The only question they have left is, "Why can I trust this person to deliver what they say they're going to deliver?"

Therefore you need to make what you're going to deliver - your promise - clear and easy to understand. This isn't a guarantee, it's not a slogan or a catchphrase. It's simply confirming to your ideal client what working with you involves and making clear what they will get out of it - the feelings, ideas or insights you will guide them to.

This can be articulated in many ways and is often about helping them overcome some of their fears, doubts or what's stopping them. You'll know best what your clients say to you in the first conversation - what are they anxious about, worrying over, or hesitating on?

For some, this can be as simple as explaining again the change they are seeking. For others, it may be confirming the thoughts, feelings or insights that you will guide them to. It may be a case of reassuring them of the support that you will offer them and the space that you will hold.

Don't be tempted to dive into the details here. Avoid simply listing the benefits of working with you, we'll get to that stage later. When you're asking someone to commit, we want to confirm what they are committing to and give them the reassurance they can to commit with confidence.

"We only sign up, pay attention to and pay for offers when what's promised is something we think is worth more than it costs, and we believe you're the best person to keep that promise. If your marketing isn't working, it's either because your promises aren't useful (and big) enough or [people] don't believe you're the one to keep them."[36]

A clearly defined promise works in two ways.

1. It helps you feel more confident about what you're asking someone to commit to so you can talk more clearly and confidently about it.
2. It helps the client work out if what you're offering is worth the commitment of their time, energy and money. It helps them balance the pricing exchange.

It doesn't have to start with "I promise to..." but it should be short enough that it confirms what the client needs to hear right before they commit.

---

[36] https://seths.blog/2012/10/useful-and-believable-promises/

For example, the promise of this book is: "In this book, you'll package up your best work, take it to the people who will benefit the most, and invite them to work with you ethically and effectively."

EXERCISE: Your promise

This is the exercise that people try to avoid, making excuses as to why they can't make a promise. This is why their marketing doesn't work.

If you are not clear on the promise you're making, how can you expect your clients to trust you to deliver it?

This is worth spending some time on.

Write down in a few sentences what promise you're making. It might take a few goes to get it right.

I would suggest going for a quiet walk (no music or podcasts) with a notepad at hand and your phone in your bag, to clear your mind and really consider:

What is the promise you're making?

40

The first step

To help prospective clients commit to working with you, the first thing to do is make sure that the first step they need to take is really clear and simple.

After nearly two decades of working in marketing, it still surprises me how many people have not gotten this simple step sorted. That's why it is the first thing I recommend people work on.

If you meet someone networking, or someone recommends someone to you, what's the first step they need to take to work with you?

This is often so simple it can be easily overlooked.

If you want someone to book a call with you, then make it easy to book a call with you. If you want someone to fill in a form and tell you a bit about themselves, then make the form easy to find and easy to fill in.

This really does seem too simple to be writing in a book but you'd be amazed at the number of websites I still find that have neither of these two things sorted.

Creating a simple first step means it's quick to reply to an email, or LinkedIn message or share in a chat message how people can take that first step in working with you.

This being said, I do not recommend just putting your mobile number or email address on a webpage. There are a lot of nasty little robots out there that will find these and send you a LOT of spam emails and calls. Instead, use a tool that makes the first step simpler and more rewarding for the client.

If you'd like people to book a call with you then consider using a call booking service. This could either be a real-person service where someone actually answers the phone, or you can use an automated service like Calendly or Acuity. Both of these tools are great because it allows someone to choose and commit to a time that works for both you and them.

If you are using a form then keep it simple. It's easy to get carried away when making a form and keep adding more and more questions. From the client's point of view, each question you add is more time and energy they need to expend to take that first step; so save the details for later and keep it simple!

Top Tip: Remember to check that your first step works on mobile devices. You might be building your website on your laptop; it's most likely your potential clients will look at your website on their phones. So make sure it works and looks good for them!

Also, if you don't get any enquiries for a while, check the form is working. Nothing on the Internet is 'set and forget'. Code changes every week and something that was working last month might now be broken. In 20 years of making websites I have yet to find an exception to this rule.

41

Why prompts

To help you start to bring together and articulate some of the notes, ideas and thoughts you've got so far we're going to use some *why* prompts.

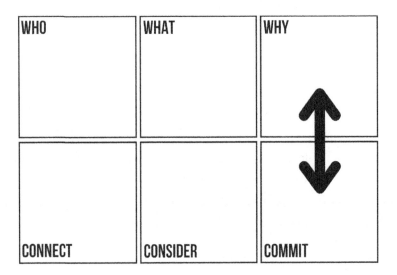

As you can see the COMMIT box is linked to the WHY box. In this next section we'll build on your *why* and articulate that to the people who are almost ready to say yes. We do this using the *why* prompts.

These questions are adapted from the book The Science of Selling by David Hoffeld; a book I read a long time ago and to be honest one that does not make my recommended reading list for a number of ethical reasons. However, I do think the question process David explains holds a lot of value for looking at your product and method from your client's point of view. So let's work through these *why* prompts.

For each prompt write a few sentences in response.

Why change?

Describe where your ideal client is now, what they are thinking, feeling and doing.

Describe where your ideal client wants to be, the thoughts, feelings and actions they would like to have or be doing.

How would they describe the change they want to make?

Why do they want to make this change?

What's stopping them?

You have already worked on this in the *why* section so you use those notes to help.

What we're doing here is making clear all the things that might motivate or inspire change. It is used to create some friendly tension.

Why now?

What might they do if they don't work with you? Describe the results of not making the change?

How would they describe what it will be like after they have made the change?

This could be from your work on their wants that you identified earlier, as well as from your notes in the *why* section.

What we're doing here is building on that friendly tension and showing that if they identified with the current situation you just described then this confirms that they are indeed in the right place.

After these two *why* prompts your client will either be thinking this isn't me, or they will be feeling like you have read their mind.

Why your offer?

Describe in broad terms why what you do works. Not necessarily your method, just in a very broad sense the work that you do. For example, coaching, mentoring, training or a course. Why does ... work?

Why is doing it or trying to do it on their own not as effective?

What we are establishing here is why working with you is more effective than going it alone.

Why you?

Describe why a client can trust you to deliver your promise. What is it about your experience, qualifications, certifications, and lived experience that makes you the perfect guide.

This is building trust in you. You have already worked on this in the *why* section so you can take elements of your story from there.

Why your method?

Describe why your method works and, if relevant, what makes it different from others. What is it about your method that will help the client get where they want to be?

This is building trust in your method and reassuring them that if they have resonated with it and understood it they can trust in it.

Why commit?

Describe why investing time, energy and money in working with you is worthwhile.

This helps to reassure people that others have invested and have got where they wanted to be. It's being honest about the work involved and the promise that you are making.

This is allowing them to make an informed decision about if they are ready to commit to the work.

Your answers to these *why* prompts will be used on your website and in your marketing content later on. It's likely you will revisit and rewrite these answers as you talk to more and more clients. Your answers will, and should, evolve over time.

42

Do I need a website?

In my experience, a website is an essential marketing tool. Some people think that they don't need a website because they're on LinkedIn, Instagram, Facebook or other social networks. Whilst it may be that the majority of your interactions are on social media and may remain on social media, there are two important things to consider:

1. You don't own the social channel, so if they decide to block or restrict your account, or if your account gets hacked - then you risk losing your online presence.
2. At some point a prospective client or someone referring you is going to Google you. Whilst currently, your social media accounts may appear in the search results, it would only take a small change in the Google algorithms for that search result to disappear.

An example of this was Twitter (now X.com). For many years Google showed tweets in their search results, so you could read tweets on Google. Then Twitter decided they didn't like this because people didn't need to go to Twitter to see the tweets, so they blocked Google. If that was your main source of new connections you were suddenly cut off.

Without a website, you are at the mercy of social media companies and their internal politics.

Website essentials

Your website doesn't have to be tens of pages packed full of text and images, it could simply be a one-pager that answers the questions of *who*, *what* and *why*, with an invitation at the bottom laying out the first step you want prospective clients to take.

You can include all the details on one page, or split them into a few different pages if you feel that works best for you. Some ideas for other pages are coming in the next chapters.

You can have different pages for your method, product and more information about you. Your website can be as simple or as complex as you want to make it.

A website is never finished, it is just the current version. You will always be coming back and updating, changing and revising the content as you learn more and your understanding of your client, product and method evolves.

At the very least your website should include:

- Your *who-what*-promise
- Your answers to the *why* prompts
- The first step you want the client to take

Rather than go into the details here, I have made a more detailed guide that explains each of these elements in more detail.

You can find it on my website: reframingmarketing.com/downloads

Am I in the right place?

When a person visits a webpage, they spend between 1-3 seconds working out if they are in the right place. So you need to help them make that decision with a very short statement that describes them and what they're looking for.

We do this with a simple **short** sentence that takes the format of: who, what, and your promise.

Your *who* and *what* are interchangeable, for no particular reason, sometimes it just flows better one way around or the other.

You can also add your promise to the end as well if you feel this makes it clearer.

The most important thing is that you can say all of this in one go with no full stops. Keep. It. Short.

For example:

- Marketing training and support that empowers coaches to attract better clients, build a bolder offer and be braver with prices, planning and purpose. (*what - who - promise*)
- 1-2-1 coaching for creative writers to get their first book published. (*what - who* - promise)
- Get clear on what's holding you back from building your coaching business. (promise - what - who)

EXERCISE: Write down your who-what-promise sentence.

This will take a few times to get right and you might go round and round in circles with it. Try a few out with clients or colleagues and see what lands with them. You can always change it if a better phrase comes up later on.

43

Commit checklist

Work through the exercises and create these elements. You might like to note down your *who-what*-promise sentence in the COMMIT box on the plan. Some of your other notes will undoubtedly be too long for the small box, so don't feel like it all needs to go in there.

- *Why* prompts
- First step - clear and simple
- Your *who-what*-promise sentence
- Create (or review) your webpage

44

BOX 5: Giving clients something to consider

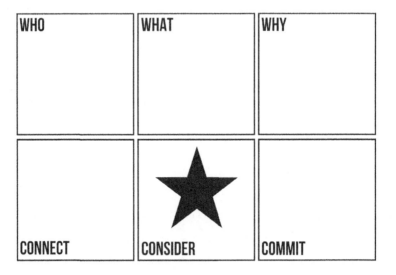

WHO	WHAT	WHY
CONNECT	CONSIDER ★	COMMIT

Now that we have somewhere to direct people to, we can begin the process of taking them on the journey to becoming a client with the next section in the marketing plan: consider.

We have set up the place they can go if they feel motivated to work with you, so now we can help someone find their way from feeling curious to inspired.

In this chapter you will work on:

- Where your ideal client is now (Present Island)
- Where they want to end up (Future Island)
- How your method can be the path in between

Your marketing is about showing the client how they can go from where they are now to where they want to be, and showing them where the opportunities for change are.

Separating out your product and your method means you can talk about the change you help people make without it being a sales pitch. It means you have somewhere to direct people to if they'd like to learn more. When you're talking on a webinar, podcast or at a networking event, it means you can talk about how your method works and some of the thoughts, feelings and insights that come up along the way - all without it feeling like a sales pitch.

In this Consider stage, we are going to help your client understand the change, and what might happen along the way so they can make an informed decision about whether this is the right change for them.

45

Where are they now?

We are building the journey for people to follow towards becoming a client. With the Commit stage ready for people to say 'yes', the next thing we are creating is a way for them to understand and contextualise what working with you looks and feels like.

To do this we need to consider what it is you think prospective clients would likely be thinking, feeling or doing in order for working with you to have the impact that is desired. You have already done some of this thinking back in the *who* chapter, so you can look back at those notes and expand on them in this exercise.

EXERCISE: Where are they now?

Looking back at your notes from the exercises in the *who* chapter, and answer these questions.

- How would you describe where your ideal client is now?
- What are they thinking, feeling and doing, and what impact is this having on their lives?
- What are some ideas, concepts or theories that are important for clients to understand, or at least have considered, before they start working with you?

46

What's the path they can take?

The next thing to do is to show them the path that they can take - your method. This helps people who are curious become inspired about the change you are describing.

The explanation of your method will take some time to get right and it will almost certainly evolve over time. The key thing that your method is doing is supporting the clients' consideration process because it allows them to align themselves with your way of thinking which only further strengthens their belief that you are the right person to guide them.

There is a common misconception that sharing everything up front will mean that clients don't need you to do the work, that they can get there on their own, when in fact the opposite is true. By giving the clients an opportunity to gain a deeper understanding and comprehension of the theories, concepts and ideas that you're going to be working on with them, it only strengthens the fact that you are the expert and are best-placed to be their guide.

In considering your method, clients can understand and contextualise what work is involved and the amount of time and energy they will need to invest in order to make the change they want to make. It helps them to get to know you and the way you work, as well as experiencing a sample of what working with you might look and feel like. It gives them an opportunity to decide if the way you work is right for them.

It also helps to shape their understanding of what their experience of doing the work might look and feel like. As they consider the different ways of getting where they want to go, one option will stand out from the others and this is the one they will seek a guide to help them with.

For example, the key concepts contained in this book are also available on the website and via social media. It doesn't stop people from buying this book. In fact, it's more likely that once someone understands the key concept of connect, consider and commit they will want to learn more, which they can do by buying the book.

The same is true for your prospective clients. If someone connects with the way that you explain or articulate your method, they're likely to want to know more about it or to experience what you are describing in person.

Just because you give people the tools doesn't necessarily mean they will do it themselves. Sometimes it can be necessary for people to try to do it themselves before they realise they can't and they need a guide to help them. Obviously in some cases a DIY approach is not appropriate and therefore you will want to explain why people shouldn't try to do it themselves in those circumstances.

To some this can feel a bit daunting, as if you're putting a flag in the ground and saying, "This is my work." This comes easier to some people than others.

Myth-busting!

Some resistance to this I hear is, "People might copy it," and, "Peers might judge me." While both may be true, both are also ok. If someone does copy the whole thing, you have some very solid ground to say that you put it out there first and prove they copied you. More important perhaps is to consider why they would do so in the first place. Think about chefs who also write recipe books. These books tell you how to cook their food yourself, at a fraction of the cost and in your own home. Their restaurants are still full as people go for more than just the assembled and cooked ingredients. The same is true with your work, people will want the experience of working with *you*.

Peers may well judge you, they probably already have and they always will. It's important to move on from this. Very few people are publicly mean or disrespectful so worrying about what they think is not worth the time or energy. As RuPaul says, *"What other people think of me is none of my business."* If they do want to talk about your method then this is good because it will open a conversation and you can learn from each other. And if there are criticisms, so what? Your work isn't for everyone and that's ok, your work is especially not for your peers, so what they think really doesn't matter. You do you.

EXERCISE: Describe how you work

When I have tried this exercise with clients and simply suggested they write down a description of their method, one of two things happens:

1. They write a few sentences then hit a block, or
2. They write pages and pages of very detailed text.

I have found the best way to describe your method is to describe it to someone else. So, this exercise is going to inspire that kind of description.

We're going to use your illustration of your method and record yourself explaining it as if you were talking a client through it.

There are a number of ways to do this, the easiest is to record it on your phone. The video doesn't have to be perfectly lit or filmed on a fancy camera, keep it simple and short. Don't worry if you stumble over your words, just keep going as if there is a client listening. If you struggle with this then you might like to try actually calling a client and recording the call (with their permission of course).

Once you have a recorded version, watch it back and see how you feel about it. Don't focus on your voice (most people don't like how their voice sounds) or how it looks - focus on your words. After watching, ask yourself would you change some of the words you used? Is it clear? If you struggle with a section, why is that? If you get lost or can't find the right word for a section, why is that and what are those words?

Then, film it again (as many times as you need to) until you're happy with how you have described it.

I then invite you to send this to a client or trusted friend and ask them what they think of your method. Remember to ask for the right kind of feedback, you don't need to know if the camerawork is good or the sound is clear. You want to know if they understand it. Does it seem manageable; like something they could work through?

This process will be quite quick for some people. For others this might take a while to get clear on. There is no rush here.

171

Once you have a version you're happy with, transcribe the video using a tool like Otter.ai or Descript and then edit this transcript until you're happy with the written version of your method.

Try not to add too much to it as you do this. Remember short and simple is best.

47

What will your client's lives be like after they work with you?

Something that is important to articulate clearly when describing your method is what your clients' lives will be like *after* they have worked with you.

I'm not suggesting you will be able to describe their future lives in detail, just in terms of thoughts, feelings and actions, how they will be different to where they are now. This is about describing in their words where they want to be, or end up. It's not about trying to define every aspect of the client's life, just to paint a picture to give them an understanding of the change that they can expect.

By being truthful and transparent and saying up front the things that you can't be certain of, or can't clearly define, you build further trust. This is all about managing the potential client's expectations of the change and allowing people to really consider whether the work is right for them, and whether the energy they're going to have to commit is worth investing.

This helps you avoid working with clients who have unrealistic expectations, or have misunderstood the change they seek to make, or underestimated the work that will be involved. It can save a lot of time spent talking to people who are not yet ready to do the work or don't see the value in it. When these people become clients, they often end up being disappointed and won't go on to refer you to others, having had what they feel is a bad experience working with you.

Contrast this with clients who really understand the process and the outcomes, insights and feelings they are likely to get by working with you. By setting expectations early in the journey, these clients will have a much better time working with you and are much more likely to go on to refer you and your work.

Once you have created content for people to truly consider what you have to offer (which we'll do next) you can then put your time and energy into connecting with your ideal client. You can be more creative with your content knowing that you have somewhere to point your audience to learn more and consider what you are offering. It means you can direct people to your website with confidence knowing that the information they seek is there, ready and waiting.

EXERCISE: What does 'after' look like?

Write a few sentences that answer these questions:

- How would you describe what 'after' looks and feels like for an ideal client? Remember to use their words wherever possible.
- How can you use this to set expectations and manage people's understanding of where they are likely to end up or get to by working with you?
- What do they think, feel and do differently?
- How might they articulate this change?

48

Creating your method webpage

The next stage is to bring together your work in this section so far into a webpage.

This will include describing where your client is now, where they want to end up and how your method can be the path in-between.

You might also like to make a video that explains all this, especially now you have had a few goes at recording it. Watching and listening to you explain your method can be a really powerful way for your ideal clients to connect with you.

Rather than go into detail here I have made a more detailed guide that explains each of these elements in more detail. You can find it on my website:

reframingmarketing.com/downloads

49

Offering something to take away

Some people will want to know even more about this method and how it works - we're all curious when something has piqued our interest.

When you first start out, this curiosity will inspire people to take the first step you have signposted them to on your webpage. After a while you may find yourself with too many calls where you are explaining the same things over and over again. When this happens, you might like to create something that goes deeper than just the webpage explanation you have created. You can create something that answers some common questions, prompts some deeper thinking, or perhaps even inspires some action for potential clients to take.

In the 'status quo' world, this is often called a lead magnet. As with a lot of standard marketing theories and practices, it shares many of the same principles with more ethical marketing but differs in its execution and intention.

What you are creating here is something for those who are curious, inquisitive or unsure. You are offering further explanation, detail and clarity for those who feel they need it before they take the first step. The idea behind this is not to leverage or manipulate their decision, rather to help bring them to a point where they feel more confident in taking the first step, or to decide that it's not right for them.

You can get creative with what it is you offer. It could be a written guide, video, email series, webinar... you name it.

A written guide might explore each stage of your method in more detail and answer some common questions. A video may do the same and might be accompanied by some prompts or questions for them to consider.

You might prefer to split the material up into a series of emails, prompts or questions that you can send to them in stages, giving them time to work on each one without overwhelming them with a big guide all at once.

You could offer a webinar where you explain this all live and answer questions from the audience.

You could offer a magical mixture of all of these. Or something completely different and unique.

Whatever you create, remember that if you want to give it away as a gift it must be truly free.

In the EU you cannot call something 'free' if you ask for an email or other personal details in return[37]. It is perfectly acceptable to ask for this information, just make sure you are being clear about the transaction that is taking place; i.e. don't say it's free.

Asking for an email in return for something is ok, as long as you're clear why you're doing so and what you will do with it. The key question to answer is, why do you need the email? Does it benefit the client, or you? Does it make the decision-making process easier for them? Would you want to receive these emails?

---

[37] EU directive – https://eur-lex.europa.eu/eli/dir/2019/2161/oj

It can be far more effective to create an email that is enticing enough for people to want to receive without relying on 'reciprocity'. It's a far better experience all round to create an interesting email that people want to receive and sign up to without swapping their information for the 'gift'. You can always offer your gift to those people who do sign up, and anyone else who is curious.

50

Consider checklist

In the CONSIDER box note down what you are offering for your client to consider (webpage/blog/video) as a reminder of where to signpost people from your content.

Work through the exercises and create these elements:

· Your method webpage (optional: video).

You might also like to create:

· Webpages, or blog posts, for the key concepts you talk about.

More detailed guide/video series/webinar for those who want a deeper dive.

51

BOX 6: Connecting with new people

WHO	WHAT	WHY
★ CONNECT	CONSIDER	COMMIT

The Connect stage is where you get creative. This is where we make your first connections with people and inspire them with ideas, prompts and invitations.

This stage of marketing is the one most people often think of as marketing because it's the most visible. This is where you are trying to catch the attention of the unaware and get them thinking, which will inspire them to find out more.

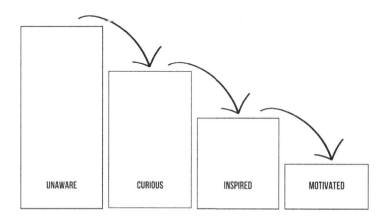

UNAWARE   CURIOUS   INSPIRED   MOTIVATED

Some of you may have noticed earlier that the cascade of clients is made up of blocks that decrease in size, as clients move along the marketing journey you have created for them. This reduction in size represents the effort required to engage with them.

The first stage, Unaware, requires the most effort to engage with people. This is primarily because they are not yet aware that this is something they should be paying attention to, thinking about, or acting upon.

Marketing feels hard when you try to move people from Unaware to Motivated in one jump. I see this when people try to explain to people they've just met why they need coaching or why someone needs to buy their 5-week course.

There are some people out there who are looking for what you're offering right now. When they show up, it feels good to have exactly what they're looking for ready to offer them. For most people, however, the journey to change takes a little longer to engage with.

It is possible to skip the queue and push paid ads on people at this time. You can pay to interrupt people and show them what you believe they need to buy. For some people this works, especially when what is on offer is 'lightweight' change. For example, offering a £50 course to learn how to optimise your to-do list is an easy sell to someone looking for a quick fix. If the change you are offering goes deeper than this, then be wary of doing what others do and pushing solutions at this stage.

A more effective way to engage people at the Unaware stage is to inspire thinking. This kind of content is more effective in the long term and will attract the kind of client who is ready to do the work, rather than those looking for a quick fix, or a shortcut.

In this chapter you will work on:

- Attracting the right people
- Making content the easy way
- What content to create
- Creating a content workflow
- Getting more referrals

In the previous sections, you have created a path to direct people towards, which means you can relax knowing that you don't have to explain how your method works or what your product is when you are first connecting with people. All of that is ready for them to discover and explore at their own pace.

Without this burden, you are free to explore new ideas, be creative with the content you produce and share, and the conversations you have.

When I talk about 'content' I am not just talking about social media posts, it can be videos on YouTube, podcasts, blog posts, a regular article in a publication, a flyer or even a brochure.

Content is most effective when you show up consistently for an aligned audience and demonstrate that if they lend you their attention, it will take them on a journey they want to go on. In telling your story and presenting prompts and questions to get them thinking, you will earn the trust you need in order for them to consider working with you.

I used to go to a networking event with Susan Payton, the storytelling expert from the *why* chapter. Every week, we'd take our turn to say what we did and who we wanted to connect with (yawn). Susan wouldn't do this. Instead, she'd share a very short story and captivate the room every single time. Her way of connecting with the audience was to show that storytelling is accessible, easy and fun. For those who wanted to tell their story better, or simply find out more about storytelling for their business, Susan was clearly the person to have a conversation with.

This chapter isn't about becoming the next social media megastar, it's about getting creative and building a habit so you can show up consistently for the people who you can serve most effectively.

52

Attracting the right people

"We ask people to eagerly lend us their attention. The promise is that it's worth their effort, because, in exchange, they're going to get the insight or the forward motion that they want."[38]

Marketing isn't about trying to get the attention of everyone, all of the time. Attention is a precious and valuable thing. So when you ask people to lend you their attention, you need to deliver something of value in return.

As Seth Godin says, *"When someone chooses to pay attention, they are actually paying you with something valuable"*[39] and people are becoming increasingly aware of how much they are 'paying' to scroll through social media apps.

People are also increasingly aware of when you have paid to interrupt them. You might have heard someone complain that a social media platform is full of paid ads.

---

[38] Seth Godin, This Is Marketing, Penguin Business 2018, 159

[39] Seth Godin, This Is Marketing, Penguin Business 2018, 190

What I hear is, "I feel like I'm being asked to give too much of my attention to people I don't want to give it to."

When you pay to interrupt people with ads, you are not getting their permission and enrollment first. So you are already at a disadvantage compared to someone who they want to engage with and hear from.

A more effective way to use content is to seek permission to engage with someone and then ask them to enrol in the journey that will unfold. The key to this is trust. We agree to go on journeys with people we trust.

We're going to look at how to create content that does this, and how to do it in a way that isn't draining or time-consuming. Instead, over time, it will become part of your regular daily or weekly routine.

53

Making content the easy way

One of the most common pushbacks I get at this stage is, "I don't want to make that type of content," or, "I don't want to use social media."

In response, my question to them is this:

How much are you willing to change to get where you want to go?

The reason for this question is simple. If you're not willing to change what you do, then you're hoping that the world will change to suit you. If what you are doing was already working, then you wouldn't need to make any changes. Therefore in order to make happen what you want to happen, you will need to get out of your comfort zone and make some changes in order to get to where you want to go. That may mean producing content and engaging with social media.

To make this change a little easier, let's look at content from another perspective. Keeping your story to yourself, not sharing the work you do and the impact you can have on people's lives is a loss for everyone.

Seth Godin describes marketing as, *"The privilege of delivering antici-pated, personal and relevant messages to people who want to get them."*[40] So, if you choose not to share your work, ideas and messages with your audience it's not just you that loses out. The world needs to hear what you have to say.

This chapter is going to help you do that, and I hope to inspire in you the confidence to give something new a try.

---

[40] Seth Godin, This Is Marketing, Penguin Business 2018, 189

54

Why you only need 100 true fans

The 'status quo' world would have you believe you need to grow a huge online audience – the bigger, the better. Social media companies tell you that to be seen as successful, you must spend a lot of time and energy chasing more and more likes and followers. The thing is, these followers/connections/friends, whatever words they use, are just part of the game. They are the status signals the social media company provides that make people want to play the status game.

The reality that social media companies don't want you to think about is this: you don't need a huge audience to make your business work. You don't need to continually interrupt people's attention to sell them things. You don't need their vanity or status metrics in order to enjoy the platform or gain status. The platform wants to make you think and feel that you do.

In 2008, Wired editor Kevin Kelly wrote an essay called 1,000 True Fans[41]. The idea is that creatives don't need to be super-famous, they just need enough superfans to make a comfortable living.

---

[41] Kevin Kelly's blog post - https://kk.org/thetechnium/1000-true-fans/

Kelly's formula was based on 1,000 people, each spending $100 a year. Since then, tech writer Li Jin has suggested 1,000 True Fans? Try 100[42], rebalancing the formula to be 100 people each spending $1,000.

Obviously, the exact numbers and amounts are fluid, depending on how much you think you need to earn for it to be a 'living'. The basic point stands: instead of trying to encourage a large number of people to engage with you a little, focus on trying to encourage a small number of people to engage a lot.

What's a superfan?

For a creative, a superfan is someone who buys everything they produce. What does the equivalent for your business look like?

- They apply what they learn from working with you to get where they want to go.
- They read and share your content.
- They download and use your guides, prompts and exercises, etc.
- If you write a book, they buy it, not just for themselves but for others too.
- And they recommend you to their friends and contacts.

What fans do for you

We're thinking beyond a fan being someone who will hand over their $100 or $1,000. When you just focus on 'getting followers', it makes your content transactional.

By shifting your focus to building a receptive fanbase - the people in your audience who are truly engaging with your content - you can

---

[42] Li Jin's blog post - https://a16z.com/2020/02/06/100-true-fans/

start the engagement earlier, focusing on those who are ready for the journey of becoming a client.

Fans are not followers.

Your followers are people who have clicked 'like' on Instagram or follow your LinkedIn account. A fan is someone who regularly engages online, comments on posts and articles, responds to polls, opens your emails, and attends events and webinars. So, for this idea to work you need to build up a base of 100 people like this who appear willing to buy at some point in the near future.

Do you need followers then? Yes, and although by default a follower is not a fan, some will be on a journey to becoming fans. So you need more followers than fans to allow for some to decide it's not for them... yet.

From my experience of opening new social media profiles for clients and watching them grow I have found that the first 100 people are the hardest to reach and connect with, after that it seems to pick up momentum and grow for as long as you consistently show up with content and engage with your network.

55

What content to create

Conversations with my clients about creating content often start with thoughts like, "Hasn't someone already said that?" and the truth is yes, they probably have. The point is, YOU haven't said it yet!

What you say and how you say it are unique to you, and if people are going to get to know you and your *who*, *what* and *why*, then they need to experience you saying it. As we have established, the world needs to hear what you have to say and the Internet allows you to say it and share it easily, cheaply and quickly.

With so many content options open to you it can be hard to know where to start. The format of your content is going to be a matter of personal preference and a balance of meeting the wants of your audience and prospective clients in terms of showing up where they are.

   If your audience watches a lot of videos on YouTube then you need to be making videos for them there, if they are avid listeners of podcasts then showing up on TikTok isn't going to be an easy way for them to find you. If you're going to go fishing, go where the fish are.

You don't have to be everywhere all at once, quite the opposite in fact. You just need to meet them where they are.

The first hurdle to overcome with content is to decide what to make content about. Knowing what content you are going to make also informs the platform and format it is best suited for it.

What to make content about

It's easy to overcomplicate content creation. You can get lost in the technical detail, the editing, the polishing or even just in a maze of ideas.

The simple way to think about making content is to ask yourself: What will get people thinking?

If you get asked the same questions regularly then make content that answers these questions (one at a time). If you find you are explaining a concept or methodology over and over then make content that explains it. If you find yourself with an idea that you want to share that you think will resonate with your ideal client then, you guessed it, make content about that.

You already have your method, product and first step laid out and ready to go. So your content doesn't have to include this, explain it or even directly link to it.

The aim of your content is to get people thinking, feeling or doing something differently. The best response to your content is, "I'd never thought of it like that before," or, "That really got me thinking," or, "I've changed the way I do this now and it's made such a difference."

When released from the burden of trying to sell or explain your product or method in every piece of content you can focus on creating something more interesting and inspiring.

Your content will resonate with your *who* when you make it specifically for those who might be experiencing the feelings, thoughts or actions that your ideal clients are experiencing. It's best to let the audience self-select if this is the right content for them. To know more about your audience and whether content is appropriate or not you need to have been specific in identifying your *who*.

For example, when I write about marketing, I focus all of my content on people doing their own marketing. I mention them in the title, in the opening paragraphs, and I'm always relating my examples to people like them. I use a level of detail that speaks about the particulars of doing marketing yourself, which means that they resonate with my content. I don't speak about how to do marketing as a marketing manager or as an agency. It doesn't mean that what I speak about won't work for anybody else, it just means that it's written specifically for people doing their own marketing.

Write and create content with your ideal client in mind. Remember to reference your ideal client, it will help them think, "They're talking about me."

New for entertainment - repetition for results

Another common misconception is that when you have said something once, you don't need to say it again. A lot of people are scared that their audience will remember that they have talked about a topic, theory or idea before, and if they mention it again people will call them out or get bored. Research tells us that the opposite is true and the harsh truth is that people don't remember your content for very long.

According to author Daniel Priestly, when creating content it's important to mix it up: *"...new for entertainment and repetition for results."*[43] So don't be afraid to cover the same topic from different angles or perspectives.

As your learning expands over time, come back to the core concept, idea or methodology that underpins and supports the change you guide people through. Explain it again, share a story about it, or use a different metaphor to talk about it.

In 2011, Google published research into what they called the Zero Moment of Truth[44]. To save you from reading some very long reports, this is a very brief summary...

On average, someone will spend seven hours researching a considered purchase, across eleven 'touchpoints' and in four different locations, before they feel confident to make their decision.

7 hours, 11 times in 4 places.

That might sound like a lot until you consider the last time you purchased a car or a house. How long did you spend researching that?

When it comes to investing in ourselves or change in our lives, I believe the same amount of research is undertaken to make an informed, confident decision.

---

[43] https://www.youtube.com/watch?v=Suzu3CrdtBw

[44] Although Google has since removed the original paper from its website, they have many newer reports on its ZMOT website: https://www.thinkwithgoogle.com/marketing-strategies/micro-moments/zero-moment-truth/

So what does this tell us about making content? Two things. Firstly, people will spend time reading, watching and engaging with things they're interested in. Think about people who binge a whole season of a TV series in one weekend on Netflix. People have the time and concentration when they are interested and engaged. Secondly, it tells us that people engage with content in different ways in different places so we need to meet them where they are, and in the format they enjoy the most.

Essentially what this means is that we're going to create the Netflix of you, so your prospective clients can binge their seven hours of content with you.

EXERCISE: Content ideas

There is a simple way to get the ideas flowing and turn them into content that your audience will engage with and share.

To start with, write down something that your ideal client is currently thinking, feeling and doing. Don't judge whether this is right or wrong just yet, just picture your ideal client sitting at home, in the office, walking in the woods or wherever, and think of one thing they are currently thinking, feeling or doing. Just one! If you have more than one, note them all down, pick one and then carry on.

For example:

- They're feeling overwhelmed by their to-do list.
- They're struggling to sleep which makes them feel drained and disconnected.
- They're saying yes to too many things and have no time to focus on what's important.

Once you have something written down, think about how they might like to consider that feeling differently in order to get from where they are, to where they want to be. We're not going to try and solve the problem or explain it in great detail. We just want to help them link these ideas, thoughts or concepts in their minds. You're aiming to spark a realisation or connection.

It can be useful to imagine you are meeting an ideal client and they ask you a question or explain where they are right now and then think about what you would suggest they do.

For example:

- Having a long to-do list can be a sign that you are a rescuer and are focusing too much on helping others rather than yourself. Here are three things you can do to identify who it is you're really helping and focus more on you.
- Lack of sleep can be linked to stress, which is also a common sign of feeling disconnected. Here are three things you can do to identify signs of stress and start to reduce them.

This is the beginning of a great piece of content because it will grab the attention of the ideal client *if* they are currently thinking, feeling or doing the thing that you're talking about. They'll be curious to know how they could do something different with that thought, feeling or action. You'll be setting up the tension for those who are there now and for those that aren't quite there yet. Maybe you'll shift them slightly closer, or perhaps it's just not for them... yet.

Just a simple act of getting someone to consider their situation in a different way or from a different perspective is enough for a piece of content.

You're not trying to solve the problem or offer the entire solution to their current situation. All you want them to do is engage with your content and think, "I never thought of it like that before."

56

Making content with AI

A lot of people are saying that AI can do your marketing for you now. This is true up to a point, AI can create your marketing content. It can write your posts, blog articles, emails, and even website copy. It can also make images and, if you're really dedicated, podcasts and even videos.

But so far, everything AI creates is, to be frank, boring. Yes, it's impressive that it can do it at all. But it's the most average of the average content out there.

This is not to say don't use it or that it can't help in a lot of ways – I use it in my marketing all the time.

But I don't use AI to do my marketing *for* me. I use AI to do my marketing *with* me.

Is it really you?

If you can't be bothered to write your own content, then why should anyone bother to read it?

I could ask an AI tool to write my blog posts and it would be done in under a minute. And they would be 'OK'; they would make sense and make a logical point. But they wouldn't be my voice. Yes, I know I can make it sound more like me by writing prompts in a way that will push it to produce something similar to my tone of voice and style but the point it will make and the argument it will give will be deeply average.

It can't be anything but average. An AI tool has been trained on all of the content out there on the Internet and all the books it has 'read' and so on. This gives it a really broad understanding, but it also waters down any opinion or viewpoint. You really have to push it to take a side; it really struggles to make a point without contextualising it. As a recent article in Wired magazine[45] points out, AI models are trained on human writing (at least, for now) and the majority of human writing is, well, average; especially on the Internet.

I still use AI tools to help me create content. I've just explained its flaws and limitations, and because I know what these are I can use it more effectively.

I don't use it to write my blog posts. I do ask it short questions if I get stuck on a thought or idea; and I use its responses as a source of inspiration, alternative perspectives, or counterarguments in my writing. It's like having a marketing or research assistant ready at a moment's notice.

I use other tools to check my writing (I'm dyslexic, so I can't check myself) and I use a number of tools to ensure what I write is readable.

---

45 https://www.wired.co.uk/article/chatgpt-fluent-bs

What often gets lost in all the debate over AI use is that it's just another tool; a specialised tool that can be highly useful within limits.

At the time of writing, AI is not good enough to be able to do it all for you, but it can assist you to get your marketing done more quickly and easily. AI technology is moving so fast though that by the time you are reading this it may well have advanced to a sufficiently competent level of ability that makes this section of the book obsolete. Either that or you are the AI reading this book in order to make yourself more powerful.

What makes your content engaging is what *you* bring to the process. It's your personal voice that makes it special and stand out from the crowd. Your story, your experience, and your examples, metaphors and way of articulating an idea are why people engage with your content – and why they choose to work with you.

Otherwise it's just generic and indistinguishable from the rest of the world, the exact opposite of what you're aiming for with marketing content. In between the clear structure and logical points, you have to add your own experiences and stories into the flow – ensure that it is your voice and not some synthetic word soup.

When you put time into making your content unique, and showing up consistently and generously, people will engage with your ideas and genuinely experience what working with you is like.

If AI does everything, then people's experience is (literally) artificial, and I'm not sure many people will be interested.

By using AI as a tool to craft your content yourself, you can show up more consistently and effectively and the time saved can be used for more creative work.

I've made a list of useful AI tools that I use on my website: simon-batchelar.co.uk/best-ethical-marketing-tools

57

How much content to make

You don't have to write pages and pages, or make epic YouTube mini-documentaries for every content idea. Your content should not be too long, or too detailed - you don't want it to feel daunting to consume (or create).

If you're writing, between 500 and 1000 words is enough. If you're making a video, three to five minutes is great. If you're recording a podcast of just you talking, then anything up to 15 to 20 minutes works.

These are not exact numbers or hard limits. They're just a guide to help you keep it simple, to stick with *just one idea or concept* for a piece of content.

Remember, you don't have to explain your method, or how these things are linked together in every piece of content, all you need to do is point them to the content on your website for them to find out more.

As the amount of content you create grows, you will be able to link back to other posts, videos or podcasts that you have made that explain or explore these different ideas in more detail.

For example, I don't have to explain every single time someone asks me, "What is ethical marketing?" I simply point them to the blog post that I wrote answering this question. Every time I write a blog post and use the phrase 'ethical marketing' I simply hyperlink that word back to that blog, so if someone is interested or curious, or maybe coming across my content for the first time, and is not aware of what I mean by more ethical marketing, they can simply click the link to find out more.

As the amount of content you have created grows you'll find that you feel the need to explain the small details less and less. You will instead focus on articulating, explaining and describing one particular idea or concept.

As your audience spends more time engaging with your content they too will deepen their understanding. If they are curious about and are the right fit for your *who*, they will naturally want to find out more and will travel along the journey you have created for them.

Your first 50 posts

Another common question that I get asked is how much content do I need to make before it starts to work? As a guide I say that the first 50 pieces of content you make are just a warm-up, it's you finding your voice and your flow. After 50 posts, two things happen:

1. You get into the flow of making the content, you find your voice and get a feel for what's working.
2. You stop counting how many you've done because you're enjoying it.

You shouldn't just blindly make content and hope for the best, nor should you stick to doing exactly the same thing in the same way 50 times and expect it to work. There is an element of experimentation with different ideas, formats and styles to see what gets conversations started and what doesn't really land. Some things will inspire a lot of comments and sharing, while others won't. There isn't really a way of knowing beforehand. After a while, you will get more of an idea as to what your audience resonates with and what leaves them flat. Likes and reactions are a good barometer for this, but interactions and conversations are the real measures of success.

58

Which format is best for your content?

Not everyone learns in the same way. How people like to absorb information differs, according to one of four broad preferences.

This is a potential problem because if you always create content in the same way, the one you're most comfortable with, you're only engaging a fraction of your potential audience.

We all have our comfort zones. When creating your content, you probably have a preferred format, and your audience has their comfort zones too. In order to connect with new people you need to cater to their preferences - enter those zones - if you're going to reach them.

Maybe you like writing blog posts. Unfortunately, not everyone is a big reader. Not everyone has time to read. What about people who like to listen to content during their morning commute? How about people who get far more from a short video than they will from your carefully crafted text?

After all, you're not creating the content for you, it's for the audience and prospective clients you seek to connect with.

In order to make content for the widest possible audience, we make content for them to watch, read, listen and do.

Often referred to as the VARK learning styles, people have different preferred ways of receiving new information:

- **Visual** - watch (e.g. a video, animation, presentation, PowerPoint)
- **Auditory** listen (e.g. a podcast, audiobook, verbal instructions)
- **Read** (e.g. a blog article, website, book, how-to guide)
- **Kinesthetic** - do (e.g. an exercise, checklist, trigger cards, workshop)

As we've already learned, people spend around seven hours researching a considered purchase, so by making one piece of content in different formats you are giving more people a way to engage with your content. You're making it easier for more people to spend seven hours with you.

59

Making a content workflow

Building on what we've covered so far, we now need to think about how we can make content that covers the watch, read, listen, do styles without being overwhelmed.

The best way to make the most content with the limited time you have is to use a 'repurposing workflow'.

Any task becomes easier with routine, and a workflow is simply a sequence of tasks, helping you set up content-making as something you routinely do.

Here is an example of my workflow to give you an idea of what works for me. Everyone works differently so you can make your own version based on your needs and preferences. This workflow takes me about two hours from beginning to end.

Repurposing workflow

- Write a blog of 500-1000 words on one topic, idea or concept.
- Record myself presenting the blog (audio and video).
- Edit the video recording for YouTube and LinkedIn.
- Edit the audio recording to create a podcast episode.
- Write a social post, which I also use as the description for the video and the podcast, as well as the wording for the email.
- Send out an email with links to all the different formats.

To get this done in an hour, I use Robbie Swale's 12-Minute Method[46] for writing the blog post. I find this keeps me on target and stops me drifting off into other topics. As the name suggests, to use this method you set a timer for 12 minutes, write and then give it a read through. Robbie then shares these posts and his process ends there, for him it's all about short and consistent content sharing which I really like. I send mine to my copy editor before I go any further - being dyslexic I'm not able to check through what I have written very well. This is what I mean about making this workflow work for you. Just because it works for someone else doesn't mean you have to follow it exactly to get it to work. Use this as a starting point and play around with it until it works for you. Start simple and slow and build from there.

Whether it's once a week or once a month, following a workflow will help you show up consistently and build your 'back catalogue' of engaging content, demonstrating your expertise in ways that are very shareable on social media.

Making content in different ways to appeal to different learning styles is more work than just sticking to your tried and tested and

---

[46] https://www.robbieswale.com/about-the-12-minute-method

comfortable marketing option. But four versions is not four times the work. The different versions in different formats are all based on the same idea. You're not doing extra research or development, you're presenting the same points in different formats. And you're broadening your appeal by bringing your content (and you!) to a much larger audience.

Put simply, by expanding your range of channels, you're becoming interesting to people who would previously have been uninterested. Not because your services aren't for them. It's because your services weren't presented in a way that attracted their attention.

Set up the right workflow for you - one that starts with your comfort zone and works from there. Once you've been through that workflow a few times, the routine aspect kicks in: your comfort and confidence grows, and the whole process takes less and less time (and becomes more enjoyable!)

Set up a routine that helps you break new ground. Give it a go, see how you get on. It doesn't have to be perfect. Maybe ask someone you trust (one or two existing clients, for example) for feedback on how you're coming across on your new channels.

Embrace all four different learning styles and you'll be pleasantly surprised by the feedback and the conversations that will flow.

What to do if you're not ready for video

When you see online videos made by people who are confident on camera and are using a pro setup, it's easy to feel like you need to match them. The pressure to show up as a pro from day one is huge.

But it doesn't have to be like this. Often, this pressure is self-imposed. From my experience, I believe it's our own limiting beliefs that hold us back. The pressure to speak confidently, with the right framing, lighting and message, combine to make video creation a hurdle that is too high for most people.

The best way to start making videos is not to make a video.

The technical side – setup, filming, editing – can seem daunting but it isn't the hardest part. The hardest part is working out what to say and how to say it. After all, slick production won't make up for empty content!

That's why I think the easiest way to start making videos is to make a podcast first.

The reason I say this is because a podcast is a chance to practise working out what to say and how to say it well without having to worry about what you look like, getting the lighting right or remembering your lines as you look into the camera. That removes so much pressure.

Your podcast doesn't have to be a half-hour-long ramble; it can simply be a short (5-10 minutes) answer to a common question.

By answering questions in this way, you will get used to articulating your ideas without the added pressure of the camera. You can use notes, not use notes, it's up to you – no one can see you.

The most important thing is that it gets you used to your own voice and the way you talk when you're explaining. It might feel a bit odd at first, but after a while, you will get used to it.

What's more, audio editing is a lot easier than video editing; especially using a tool like Descript[47] – it transcribes your audio into a document and you edit the audio by simply editing the document.

As you practise editing – knowing you can always chop it out later if you stumble or lose your train of thought – you will find that you get better at 'presenting'. How you articulate your ideas improves and you become more confident. The more you do, the easier it gets.

---

[47] Find out more about this and many other useful content creation tools on my website: simonbatchelar.co.uk/best-ethical-marketing-tools

60

Being brave

If you're going to make a change then it's time to get out of your comfort zone and put yourself out there - with some self-compassion of course. Some people look at making a video or recording a podcast and think, "I can't do that." A lot of people struggle with this, so let me ask you:

What is really stopping you?

Imagine your inner critic sitting opposite you. Think about what they're saying. Are you catastrophising? What does the worst-case scenario feel like and what might it teach you? What is the evidence?

Imagine the light bulb moment - the spark of an idea, the realisation of two ideas joining in a person's mind - the moment they realise that YOU have explained something like no one else has done before. How does that make you feel?

You have the power to make an impact on people's lives and the world around you. The world needs your ideas, they want to hear your voice.

61

How do you make your content 'shareable'?

Let's think about why people might share your content - it's linked to status. People share something they like because it raises their status. They do so because they want people to be inspired or motivated, or find the same things funny that they do. They want confirmation in their belief about that content, and to feel like they have made someone else feel the same way and thus raise their status, even just a tiny amount.

If you make your content that is all about you (i.e in order to raise *your* status) then it becomes harder to share because you are asking people to promote you to say, "Please help me raise this person's status." If you make content that is generous (i.e. focused on your ideal client's situation) then it is easier for people to share because you are helping them raise *their* status. When you make content, make it for them, not you.

62

Email marketing

Email marketing often feels like yet another thing you *have* to do. I am aware I have just spent this chapter explaining lots of things you can do to create content and you might already be feeling like you have plenty to do already.

So why am I adding email to your list?

I believe it's worth the investment. Once it's set up, it builds slowly over time to become a really powerful marketing tool that scales without needing a lot of extra work from you.

Email marketing is not about the size of your list. Nor is it about the technology you use. It's about the emails you send. And yet, the technology, and growing your list of contacts, is what most people think of when it comes to email marketing and it's what they spend the most thought, effort and time on.

It's easy to get caught up in the technology behind email marketing these days because it's so good – and simple to use – that getting set up is actually the easiest part.

The biggest challenge with email marketing, and where your focus should lie, is what to put in the emails you send.

Luckily you've already got that bit sorted, because you're making content that your audience wants to hear about. An email is a great way of sending this content to your audience without worrying about a social media algorithm not getting your post in front of the right people.

Why send marketing emails?

Why emails? Why not just stick with paid ads and other 'saturation' techniques?

For a start, emails can feel more personal – after all, the email is addressed *to* the reader. It's also 'at their convenience' – the reader chooses when to read it, unlike ads.

What's more, the email is in their inbox because they chose to receive it; they signed up to your list.

Email lists are the best signal someone can give you that they want to hear from you. When they sign up they are saying "I want to hear directly from you". They are trusting you with direct access to their attention. No social network offers this.

And for you, it's easier to track the impact and results of email marketing. There are plenty of metrics: delivery rates, bounce rates, unsubscribe rates, click-through rates, open rates, etc.

But remember, people are busy

People get a lot of emails. Most of us get too many. This means you're competing for attention and you need to deliver something interesting that people *want* to read.

If you take the time to write it, most people will take the time to read it... so long as it's brief, to the point, and useful to the reader.

People who can see the work that's gone into writing an email will usually engage with interesting, short ideas that make them think.

Many of the emails I receive are focused on the person sending them, not me, the reader.

The content tells me how great this person is or how much they have achieved but there is rarely a story or topic of interest to me. This is why the unsubscribe button in my inbox gets used a lot.

When you write your emails, remember you are not the focus of the email. Sure, you will appear in the content, but "I just emailed to tell you how great I am," rarely makes for an interesting read.

The idea is to give, not ask or sell. Your email should offer something relevant to them that they can't get on social media more easily or quickly.

News is good and can be interesting, but it's not the main attraction. Remember, no one is interested in people who just talk about themselves.

Consistency beats length

Long emails tend to be a turn off. You don't have to solve everyone's problems or answer every question in every email. If people want more, they'll go to your blog, podcast, YouTube channel, or read your book.

Not everyone will read the whole email every time you send it. That's fine. Remember, people are busy.

Getting into the habit of sending consistently works for both you and your readers. Your audience will start to anticipate your emails; they're expected and – after a while – welcomed.

Regular sending also helps you keep your emails short and to the point. You don't have to say everything in each email, there's always the next one. And if people miss one, they know they can catch up next time. This builds trust and connection.

Consistency is key: consistently interesting and consistently useful. If you can nail that, the length and format can be adapted to suit the specific idea or message you're sharing.

Make it engaging

As I say, don't try to give the reader everything in each email. A detailed lecture is not right for the email format. Keep it short and digestible enough to read while standing in line at the post office.

You just need enough to get their attention. People love a rabbit hole to explore – all your email has to do is get them curious enough about a relevant topic and they'll go deeper.

Also, people don't share 'average' content or stuff they already know. They share useful, inspiring material; and sometimes trivial fun! If your email is interesting then it will be effective.

Don't explain everything

It's better to pose an intriguing question than to try and give all the answers.

This is not easy. After all, you have the 'curse of knowledge'; you know the answers already and it's tempting to share them (maybe even show off).

This can be overwhelming for the potential client. A better approach is to simply ask a relevant question or present an idea and let the reader think about the answers they need for themselves. The purpose of your email marketing is not to solve problems, it's to engage with the reader.

By all means, point them to the next step down the rabbit hole – you can write a blog post or record a podcast or video that goes into more detail, with a link from the email.

The key to email marketing is to keep it short and get the reader thinking.

63

Go networking

Marketing is not all about social media. There is a lot to be said for networking in its many forms.

I used to hate networking. I felt it was a waste of time and I didn't meet anyone who was a good fit to become a client. So I didn't go back.

Then a coach I was working with helped me reframe networking (that's an idea for my next book!) and see that I'd been doing it wrong.

I have been to some really bad networking events over the years. Sadly, there are a lot of them.

I believe one of the reasons people don't get on with networking is that they're trying to get something out of it that networking is not supposed to deliver.

Networking isn't about selling or meeting clients; it's about building your network of people who know, like, and trust you to be the go-to person for the work you do. So, if you go networking, it's not about getting leads. That might be a happy bonus every now and then, but what's really important is building a network of people who will recommend you.

64

Find your people

I go to a lot of in-person networking, but I also do some online networking. Not all of the events or forums I go to label themselves 'networking'.

For example, I am part of Like Hearted Leaders, an online community call that happens every Friday morning. It's as simple as that, like-minded people join a call every Friday and talk about a different topic in a small group. There are no sales pitches, no intros, just conversation.

There are lots of groups, communities and networking events out there. Some will support you and your business, others will be a network of peers, others will be a mixture of lots of different types of businesses of all shapes and sizes.

If you're not showing up in different places then people can't get to know, like and trust you; and they can't recommend you if they don't know you.

Just because in-person networking works for me doesn't mean it will for you. Some of my clients live in places where there are no networking groups, so they go online. Others have started the kind of group they would want to join.

65

Content checklist

Make a short list of content ideas that you can make. You might like to note some down in the CONNECT box. You might like to use another tool to organise your ideas.

I suggest a long list of ideas and a short list with just the two or three ideas that you are going to focus on next. This helps avoid the overwhelm of seeing a massive to-do list of ideas.

Here are some prompts to get you thinking:

- What questions can you answer?
- What stories can you share?
- What interesting things can you put out there that your audience might also enjoy?
- Who can you celebrate?
- What are the next three pieces of content you are going to create and when are you going to share them?
- At what stage can you ask for referrals in your work?

VI

Making the plan work - over and over again

66

Making it work for you

WHO	WHAT	WHY
CONNECT	CONSIDER	COMMIT

Now it's time to take a step back and look at all the work you have done.

If you have been working on each section as you read through the book, then you may have already created a number of webpages and pieces of content already.

If you have read through the book without doing the exercises, then now is the time to make a start. I would suggest going back to the *who* chapter and working through the book again with your deeper understanding gained from the first time around.

Whichever way you read the book, well done for getting all the way through it. I hope that the future you will be grateful you did.

67

Why are there no timings for this plan?

You may have noticed that I don't talk about how much, often, or long this will take. The simple reason for this is that after years of making my own plans, and helping others make theirs, I came to the realisation that overplanning is often a way of putting off doing the tasks in the plan.

What I mean by this is that I can't make a one-size-fits-all plan. So, this plan is the foundation for your marketing. Exactly how you get creative and show up to your audience is up to you to plan and commit to. I believe this template plan makes that easier and gives you the freedom to be more creative.

"The real problem isn't planning. It's that we take our plans to be something they aren't. We treat our plans as though they are a lasso thrown from the present around the future in order to bring it under our command. But all a plan is – all it could ever possibly be – is a present moment statement of intent."[48]

---

[48] Oliver Berkman, Four Thousand Weeks, The Bodley Head 2021, 123

Your plan is good enough. Aim to be consistent over frequent. Start slow and build up. Share generously, inspire and make people curious.

How to avoid overplanning

It's tempting to create a huge and ambitious plan that includes every single thing you want to do with marketing for the next year. I've seen these enormous plans many times before, and even created a few in my time.

Drawing up a list of things to do is the best way to avoid doing the list of things.

If you are looking at a long list, my challenge for you is to pick three things from it, work on them and then come back and choose another three.

You can spend time making a list or doing the list. It's far better to work on a few things now and then come back and work out what to do next. The things you need to do will still need to be done when you finish the first three. They might even have changed.

If you're a calendar person, set a reminder to come back and revisit the chapters in this book you want to work on more. Then set new reminders each month.

Revisit and revise

Once you have worked through each of the boxes once, and created some content and shared it with your audience, it's worthwhile reviewing and revising. Marketing is never finished.

Taking each box in turn, make a list of the things that you want to update, start over, or still need to do. Look at your plan and make your list in this order:

- Who
- What
- Why
- Commit
- Consider
- Connect

As tempting as it is when you review to skip the earlier sections, or just assume they're still right, it's often the small subtle shifts in the earlier stages that inform the most effective changes. Spending time looking again at your *who*, *what* and *why* after you have had conversations with clients and engagement with your content can really help make your marketing more effective. It will help make your content resonate even more and inspire ideas about what to create next.

Repeat and repurpose

There is a common misconception that every bit of content has to be new, or original. This is not the case, as we learned in the repetition for results section.

Your audience does not remember your content for long. You can repeat yourself often and people are unlikely to notice, and if they do they will likely feel reassured that they are starting to understand it better.

I'm not saying posting the same thing word for word will work. You can explain the same idea or concept in a number of ways, with different examples, metaphors or stories. The more you can get your audience thinking, connecting the dots in their minds and curious to know more, the better.

People won't remember that you posted something a few months ago, it might seem familiar to them, but they will most likely feel good about that. The people who are the right fit will want to know more.

People aren't making a list of what content you create, so mix it up, and go over it again in a different way. Most of all, give something new a go and keep returning to the fundamentals of your work to make sure they still say what you want them to say.

Not everyone will read everything you create. And even if they do, you're allowed to change and evolve your business over time.

There is endless advice on how often to post and how to beat the algorithm to get more people to see your posts. Rather than focusing on this, channel your energy into showing up consistently rather than frequently. Those who resonate with what you are saying will be thankful you do.

68

Getting more referrals

A lot of people say that they get most of their business from word-of-mouth referrals. They tend to think of this as being the primary, or often only, form of marketing that they need.

If that's you, you're lucky.

The problem with relying on word-of-mouth marketing is that essentially what you're doing is hoping that by doing a good job, people will talk about you and more clients will come your way. It's the business equivalent of a free lunch, lovely when you get one and you appreciate it, but you can't really rely on it to feed you.

This is not to say that referrals aren't a great way of marketing. They are. It's just that relying on them is perhaps a bit too optimistic. Being realistic gets you more clients, and without so much uncertainty.

So, realistically, how can you orchestrate more referrals – rather than waiting for that free lunch?

In order for someone to refer you, three things need to happen:

- They have to notice that a conversation they're in is about the specific area you work in.
- They have to think about you.
- They have to introduce you into the conversation, and ultimately introduce you to the person they're talking to.

That's a lot to rely on to get a referral. And it's asking a lot of the referrer.

How to actively generate referrals

In order for someone to refer you that person needs to be able to answer these three questions:

- *Who* will I tell?
- *What* will I tell them?
- *Why* will I tell them?

So one of the most effective ways to get referrals from your audience and clients is to help them answer these questions. Some people will be able to do this on their own from your website and content. They might have already worked with you or met you so they may be clear about your *what* and *why*, they're just waiting until they find a good fit for the *who*.

Some people might need a bit more help or prompt to encourage referrals. Luckily this is reassuringly simple. The best way to get referrals is to ask for them.

That might seem a bit simplistic so let's break down the 'ask' into its essential components:

- Ask at the right time – this depends on who you're asking – with a satisfied client when you're finishing up the work is a good time, arguably this is when they are most satisfied! If you're asking past clients then don't ask everyone at once - otherwise you could end up with a rush of referrals.
- Be specific about *who* it is you're looking to work with – describe your ideal client to help potential referrers choose who they will recommend you to.
- Explain the kind of situation your ideal client might find themselves in and the outcome, feeling or insight you deliver.
- Send referrers something of value like a guide or piece of content to pass on.
- Consider some form of reward for successful referrers.

This method enables the referrer to add their own personal recommendation on top of the thing of value that they're passing on. It makes them feel good.

It also allows the recipient to review your guide/website/content before they get in touch. This feels a lot less pressured than the common email intro which puts you and them immediately in a position of pressure to talk, even if the timing isn't right for them. Allowing them first to find out more about you and your work, saves you from having conversations with people who are not the right fit. Some people might not act straight away. This method allows them to approach you when they feel ready to do the work.

To ensure that you're ready to receive referrals you need to make sure they're being referred to someone that is the right fit. This means your website, guides, social content, etc. all need to be aligned.

When they clearly explain what you and the client can work on, and the outcome, feeling or insight that you guide them to, it makes it much easier for people to refer others to you.

Here's my invitation to you.

- Who can you ask for a referral?
- How can you make asking a regular part of your process or schedule?

69

Forming a marketing habit

"The market has been trained to associate frequency with trust. If you quit right in the middle of building that frequency it's no wonder you never got a chance to earn that trust."[49]

The logic seems simple – show up consistently and people will see you as dependable and recommendable. The practice is harder because it takes time, effort and a lot of repeating yourself.

It can be easy to get bored, or think that you are being boring, because you are talking about the same things over and over. Smart people get bored by repetition. As we have established though, people need to hear things many times before they notice and begin to understand them. So just because you feel bored or see yourself as a broken record doesn't mean you should stop. Remember – new for entertainment and repetition for results.

There is, of course, a balance to be made. Just repeating the same thing over and over verbatim won't work. People will spot that and lose interest. The same picture, the same phrase, the same words can

---

[49] Seth Godin, This Is Marketing, Penguin Business 2018, 177

be a drain on people's attention, which they have lent you to see if they can trust you to use it wisely. This is why paid ads can be ineffective because it's the same thing over and over and it becomes clear you are simply paying to interrupt someone's attention, which sends mixed messages.

To deliver something that is worth paying attention to takes a bit of creativity. You can revisit the same idea, topic or concept again and come at it from a different angle. You already do this without even thinking about it when you explain something to many different people; the words you use, the analogies you think up on the spot are different. You can use the same thing with your content.

Frequency is often confused with consistency. No one has a date in their calendar when your newsletter is going to be sent, yet they will be happy when it arrives. The frequency of your posts is less important than the consistency of the content. If you show up five times one month and two the next that's ok. As long as what you show up with is worth paying attention to.

A lot of people will tell you it's the other way around. They will insist that you have to post a certain number of posts, at a certain time, on certain days in order to 'win'. That's all just a game of status. The platforms will all say the more you post the better it works, but they would say that, they have shareholders to keep happy and increasing users' time spent in the app is how they do that.

Most people don't open their social app wondering what their accountant had for lunch, they do so because they want to *feel* something - what that feeling might be is a book in itself! If you show up there often enough they will either notice you or scroll on by, you don't have any control over that. When you shift your focus from views, likes and followers to conversations started you can really start to see what works and what doesn't. You might find that a certain way of explaining, discussing or illustrating really captures people's attention. Other ways might not.

"Forget about goals, focus on systems instead. Winners and losers have the same goal. If you completely ignored your goal and focused only on your system would you still succeed?"[50]

I'm not here to tell you when and how much to post. What I am here to do is to encourage you to make a manageable plan of ideas, stories and interesting things to share and see what happens.

---

[50] James Clear, Atomic Habits, Random House Business Books 2018, 24

70

How to do marketing when you have no spare time

"It's not that we have too little time to do all the things we need to do, it's that we feel the need to do too many things in the time we have"[51]

You're busy, I'm busy, everyone is busy. In many societies, we equate being busy with being successful or valued. So it's easy to be lured in by the cult of busy. It's not for me to judge how you use your time or tell you how to use it better. For a deeper dive into that world, I'd recommend Oliver Burkeman's book, Four Thousand Weeks, which explores many of our held beliefs and misconceptions about time far better than I would.

One idea I'd like to share is a reframing of the concept of being too busy to do something.

In a sense, when you choose to do Task A instead of Task B, you're saying, "I am choosing to prioritise Task A," or, "I am choosing to not prioritise Task B." When you find yourself thinking or saying, "I don't

---

[51] Gary Keller, The One Thing, John Murray 2013, 46

have time to do...," I invite you to reflect on where and how you are currently using your time and reframe it as a decision about priorities.

Ask yourself if you're focused on the right things. Is there something you could (or even should) stop doing so you can start doing what you want to do?

It's easy to look at others and judge that they're wasting their time or using it inefficiently. It's not always so easy to find that clarity when looking at your own behaviour.

For example, one common 'time drain' is something your phone has trained you to do without even thinking: scrolling through social media apps. It's called 'internet brain', as defined by Brad Stulberg:

"Internet brain results from spending too much time on the Internet. It manifests as an inability to focus for long periods of time; a strong desire to 'check' something — be it social media, email, trending topics, or your favorite newspaper's landing page — even, and perhaps especially, when you don't actually want to; a constant feeling of adrenaline that is somewhere between excitement and anxiety; a lack of patience for anything that is inherently slow; and a significantly harder time being present in offline life, such as constantly needing to pick up your phone."[52]

If this sounds like you then remember you're human, and these apps are weapons-grade dopamine dispensers. Social networks have invested hundreds of millions of dollars to get you to open the app, start scrolling, and keep on going. Their business model is based on getting you addicted, so don't feel bad about the time you spend scrolling.

---

[52] https://bstulberg.medium.com/internet-brain-is-a-real-thing-aee1d740abd2

There's no judgement here – just an invitation to re-evaluate your concept of 'busy' and how you are framing your time.

The reason I chose scrolling as the example is that we've talked about making content for these very platforms. The time you spend consuming content could be spent making content. What I'd like to suggest here is not 'delete the app'; instead, approach it with a clear intention and set some boundaries around it. These will be personal and different for everyone.

For example, one thing you can do is set an app timer to limit the time you can access the app each day. If you know you'll simply turn this off, you could even set the timer with a parental lock and ask a trusted friend or partner to set the passcode so you can't bypass it.

Alternatively, it can be interesting to consider how much you 'pay' the social app for using it. "But Facebook/X/Instagram/etc. is free," I hear you say.

Here is a simplistic calculation to illustrate my point. Let's say you charge clients £100 for an hour-long session. If you spend an hour a day on a social media app then you have effectively 'paid' them at least that amount in lost earning time, just to scroll.

You can ask your phone to tell you how much screen time you spend on your most-used social app and do a rough calculation for yourself (I suggest you sit down when you do this).

Personally, I schedule 'do not disturb' time on my phone, giving me periods of the day when my phone just sits silently (it will still ring in an emergency). After years of doing this, it still works for me... and the Internet is always there waiting for me when I return.

Anti-hustle culture

The other side to not having (making) time is swinging too far the other way and pushing so hard you risk burning out. Often referred to as 'hustle culture', its believers have seemingly endless amounts of time. They explain this by talking a lot about how they use productivity hacks and routines that are timed to the second to maximise their working time.

This cult of productivity is almost certainly nonsense, being put on for the camera. Most will be using hidden teams and subcontracting to make them appear superhuman and make you feel bad for not keeping up. They then leverage this to sell you their 'magic formula for success'.

Marketing can work even if you don't put every waking hour into it. You don't have to 'smash every day' or 'fake it till you make it'.

Make the time you can, when you can and remember to look back at what you have achieved as often as you look forward at what you have to do.

In summary, it's not that you don't have the time; it's that you're spending time on something else. Finding the right balance can take a while and whatever plan you make needs to allow for the reality that life sometimes gets in the way.

VII

Lessons from 20 years doing marketing

71

Mini Rants

In order to make this book flow better, there were a lot of sections that I cut out. I felt that some of these would be good to include as short 'rants' or riffs, as they are useful in answering some of the follow-up questions you may have after working through the process. So I have included them here.

Paid ads are a shortcut

Paid ads used to work, they used to work very, very well. Household names became household names through TV, radio and newspaper advertising. Then new gatekeepers emerged to overtake the old ones.

Google, Apple and Meta became multibillion-dollar companies by controlling access to their users' attention and decision-making processes. They make most of their money by selling access to that attention in tiny chunks to the highest bidder.

They got greedy and built vast empires, all based on selling their users' attention. Now those online spaces are filled with noise, and people's attention turns to where there are fewer paid ads.

"The shortcut [of] using money to buy attention to sell average stuff to average people is an artefact of another time, not the one we live in now."[53]

If you jump straight into setting up paid ads, chances are you'll be targeting the wrong people at the wrong time. Your paid ads will bring people who aren't ready to buy to a site selling something they don't want.

"The lifetime value of a new [client] rarely exceeds the cost of running the ads necessary to get the new [client]."[54]

So if advertising alone won't get you the clients you want, how do you cultivate them through marketing?

Paid ads can help you 'jump the queue' and get some purchases/clients without taking them on a journey. But will the people who make that quick purchase be willing to do the work? That is unlikely.

A Facebook ad might get someone who has no idea they even have a problem or an opportunity for change to click BUY in a matter of seconds, but will they be willing to personally invest and do the work? I think deep down you know as well as I do that they won't.

Better clients come when you're not trying to jump the queue.

The process in this book takes time. So does your work. If what you offer isn't a quick fix, why should marketing be?

The key is to meet the person where they are, not where you'd like them

[53] Seth Godin, This Is Marketing, Penguin Business 2018, 11

[54] Seth Godin, This Is Marketing, Penguin Business 2018, 210

to be. Then lead them to a place where they can make an informed decision about working with you. They, and you, will get much more out of it in this way.

Complex funnels

Marketing funnels have the great advantage of looking really simple. The principle behind them is that more people enter at the top than leave at the bottom.

For many years, I used the marketing funnel to illustrate how people became clients and customers. The basic principle of the funnel is sound, and I think there is a lot to be said for making a marketing process simple. However, many marketing funnels, sales funnels, training books, videos and courses seem to take the simple funnel process and make it incredibly complicated.

Some people also like to attach numbers to their funnels and use complex formulas to create important-looking percentages for each stage of the funnel. While this may work for e-commerce sales or off-the-shelf services, for most businesses this level of measurement simply isn't accurate enough for these percentages to mean anything. The main problem with complicated funnels is that they force you to focus on conversions and, as you now know, you don't want to chase conversions.

These complex funnel tools and formulas are not interested in building relationships or starting conversations, they are all about minimising human contact and automating as much of the marketing process as possible to maximise return on investment.

Of course, if (when) you find that your funnel isn't working, it's easy to blame the stage of the funnel above or below it. Or, if the whole thing isn't working, you blame the ads you're running. For this reason, they are very useful in marketing and advertising agencies as a tool to help 'explain' poor-performing campaigns.

The marketing funnel is a useful graphical tool, but it is not a strategy or a magic formula for generating sales.

Squeeze pages

There's a strange concept in the marketing world called 'squeeze pages', sometimes called 'landing pages'. The idea is to create a psychologically manipulative page that creates a false sense of urgency and scarcity, combined with fear-inducing language to leverage a sale. They are usually very long and contain lots and lots of videos, ebooks and courses.

The one thing to remember when you are reading about how effective squeeze pages are, is that you are actually on a squeeze page.

The most successful squeeze pages are the ones that sell courses on how to create squeeze pages.

There will undoubtedly be examples and case studies that show that using manipulation and tricks is more effective than not using such tactics. Squeeze pages can be very effective as long as you're comfortable working with clients you've tricked or pressured into buying what you're selling.

As we've established, if you're interested in more ethical marketing - if the kind of clients you want are not those who feel conned into buying your services - then you don't want to create a page that does exactly that.

SEO

In the early days, the Google search engine gave everyone the same results. It was very easy to game those results, and some people made a lot of money telling people exactly how to do so. It didn't take long for Google to fix the way people were gaming the system.

In recent years, Google has gone one step further and now personalises search results for each individual user and search. This makes trying to game the results irrelevant, because the results are different for every search. No two search results will be exactly the same.

Some people got used to making money by telling people how to play the game. They created a label to sell it to other people: search engine optimisation, or SEO.

SEO is alive and well today and if you pay someone enough they will tell you how to get amazing SEO results and then explain why they didn't happen.

I'm not saying SEO isn't possible, it is, just not in the way I see most SEO people talking about it.

In the world of e-commerce, there are still a lot of really effective ways to get your products to appear in more relevant searches (that's another book!)

However, if you're not selling off-the-shelf products, a lot of SEO advice simply won't work. Seth Godin shares a simple way to reframe the idea of SEO.

"Make a product or service people care enough to search for specifically. You cannot win in a generic search, but you'll always win if the search is specific enough."[55]

You can do SEO yourself and improve where you appear in search results. However, it can be a challenge. Trying to be found for a generic search term like 'life coach' or 'consultant' is beyond the reach of most people. There are thousands and thousands of pages of results returned for searches for these generic terms.

A better way to think about SEO is to be specific enough that when someone searches for that very specific thing, you come up. The easiest way to do this is to create content that answers the questions people ask you most often. These questions are likely to be specific to the work you do and the clients you work with. By answering them, you will be creating very specific content that will be the perfect match for very specific searches.

The chances are that you will be one of the very few people to have answered that very specific question, which means that you are likely to appear near the top of search results for that specific question. The added benefit is that someone who has asked that very specific question is likely to be in the process of researching it and is more likely to be on a journey to becoming a client. So while you may not get a lot of clicks, the ones you do get are from people looking for the specific answers you can help them with.

---

[55] Seth Godin, This Is Marketing, Penguin Business 2018, 178

Email marketing

Email is an often underestimated marketing channel. Email is direct access to someone's attention. As a result, people guard their email address closely.

So, if you are sending emails as part of your marketing campaign, make sure they are the kind of emails people want to open.

If you send emails that share generously, your email open rates will be higher because they will be relevant and of interest to your ideal client.

If you send emails that simply sell or push your agenda, your open rates will be lower.

The best thing about email is that people who aren't interested can unsubscribe, which means you're not wasting their time and it's not costing you money to send them more emails. Unsubscribing is a good thing - it's not personal, it's just email.

The other good thing about email is that you own the email list. Unlike 'followers' or 'connections' on social media, which are owned by the social media platforms. You own your list of email addresses. So, for example, if you use MailChimp or Drip, the email list within that programme is yours and you can take that list and move it to another platform. There are some platforms that don't allow you to do this, so be careful about building an email marketing list within a restrictive platform.

What should you be sending to your email list? The answer to this question is simple. What would your ideal client like to receive in their inbox? What will make them think? What will prompt or invite them to take action? Experiment with some ideas and see what works. Instead of focusing on numbers like open rates and clicks, which are not 100% accurate, focus on how many people email you back or tell you they enjoyed your email.

One last point, don't call it a newsletter, nobody enjoys receiving a newsletter. People don't subscribe to newsletters because they sound boring and take a long time to read. Get creative and think of a way to package what you want to share with your audience in a way that makes them curious. For example, 'weekly prompts', '5 things I found this month', or 'inspiration in your inbox'.

Social media

"Facebook and other social media platforms seem like a shortcut because they make it appear easy to reach new people. But the trade-off is it's not your land, you don't have permission to contact people, they do, you don't own that asset, they do."[56]

Your audience and your prospective clients are on social media. After working with hundreds of small businesses, I have yet to meet one whose clients have not been on social media at some point during the day.

You may have your own preconceptions and reservations about a social media channel. You may have an assumption about what content is there and what conversations are happening.

---

[56] Seth Godin, This Is Marketing, Penguin Business 2018, 191

Regardless, if your clients are using it, they are engaging with the content and participating in the conversations. So, if you want to meet new clients, you need to be there to connect.

- You don't have to be on all of them.
- You don't have to be on them all of the time.
- You don't have to try to keep up with influencers or other people who seem to live on social media.

You can repurpose your content to fit a social media channel, however, what you create there stays there. Wherever possible, try to make your website or blog the source of your content and direct people there to find out more. Investing too heavily in one channel and keeping all your content there can be a risky strategy, as it will fall out of favour over time.

Inviting people to join your mailing list or subscribe to your blog gives you much more control over how you engage with them. It also makes you less dependent on algorithms or changes in social media trends.

Trying to be everywhere at once is exhausting, so rather than trying to be on every channel, get one social media channel up and running first and then move on to another. As we have seen in creating a habit, it is important that you are regular and consistent with your message to build trust.

Most importantly, if you feel it's not working or you're not really enjoying it, move on to something else. Don't judge this by likes and followers as a barometer of how well your message is resonating with your audience. Instead, look at how many people are commenting, sharing or messaging you about the content you're sharing. Creating conversations is the best outcome from any social channel.

Write a book

When I first thought about writing a book, I thought it would be a lot of work. Then I watched an interview with Rob Fitzpatrick who explained that writing a book has never been more accessible and manageable. I ordered his book, Write Useful Books, which explained everything I needed to know and gave me the confidence to get started. You are now reading the result of that work.

I can't say it will be easy for you, but I would recommend going through the process of writing a book as a great way to get clear about what you are doing and who you are doing it for. In doing so, you will create a great way for people to understand why they can trust you to deliver.

For more information and inspiration, visit Rob's website:

writeusefulbooks.com

My favourite sales question

The last point I want to make in this book is about a fantastic sales question that was once gifted me by sales trainer, Andy Bounds.

It doesn't use pressure or manipulation, it simply turns the conversation on its head and gets the client to explain the other side of the story. You use this question when the client is unsure or feels uncomfortable saying yes. You can even use it when they say no.

The question is: **What will you do if you don't do this?**

This question is brilliant because it invites the client to articulate what the alternative is and how they plan to do it on their own or with someone else. When this happens, you learn more about what the client perceives as a 'want' – and who better to tell that story?

More often than not, this question reveals that they don't have a plan, or that the plan they have isn't very attractive. They may then see that the best plan for them is to join a guide – you.

72

My offer to you

I enjoyed writing this book, and I hope you have enjoyed reading it.

I send regular emails with marketing prompts to inspire you to mix up your content, build your audience and fanbase, and reach the clients you really want to work with. You can sign up to get these emails and find lots of other resources on my website:

reframingmarketing.com

I also work with clients on a 1-2-1 basis and you can book a call with me using this QR code.

73

Appendix

The 5 levels of awareness

When you illustrate to the client the journey that they're going to go on, you're being transparent about the amount of time, energy and effort that needs to be invested. You're also being realistic about where the client is going to end up. It means you're not making false promises, or over the top claims about the effectiveness of your method. It also allows you to be truthful, in the sense that you are starting from a point of empathy, of understanding where the client is now and where they might like to get to.

In traditional marketing, the information flow is one way: from the person trying to persuade towards the person being persuaded. Instead of persuasion, it's more effective to focus on engagement, on asking, on listening.

In order to speak to a client in a way that doesn't feel like selling, you need to ask questions, inspire ideas or invite a change of mindset. Get them thinking about the kinds of things you work on with clients and guide them to a place where they feel that working with you is the perfect next step for them.

When you start a conversation, you make them think – with information, a question, a fresh perspective – and leave them wanting to know more.

Levels of awareness

Many people find attracting new clients hard work. They're often comfortable talking about what they do, their product or service, and explaining everything, in detail, yet struggle with the shift from prospective client to actual client.

Why does this often feel like hard work? Put simply, you're talking about the wrong thing. You're trying to take them all the way from 'barely aware they have a problem to solve' to 'buying your product' in a single leap. It's too much.

With your existing knowledge and years of experience, the process and product you offer may feel and seem obvious to you, however, a client is often starting at a point of (blissful) ignorance – they're not even aware that they have a problem, that there is an opportunity for change, or in fact that working with a guide is even an option. When there's a mismatch in understanding or awareness, jumping too quickly to 'close the deal' doesn't feel right.

By looking at the journey to becoming a client in terms of five levels of awareness, we can split up the marketing messaging and content to appeal to different stages of the journey. That way, you're addressing the prospective client's specific level of awareness, and not overwhelming them or trying to push them too fast.

The theory behind the journey people go on when considering making a purchase is very old – it was published in 1966 by Eugene Schwartz, whose copywriting reportedly sold over a billion dollars' worth of products. He wrote Breakthrough Advertising, the book that informs most of the advertising you see in your daily lives and is likely the reason you have purchased most of the stuff you now own.

Although you're not trying to sell cars, vacuum cleaners or fizzy drinks, these levels of awareness still apply. You can use them to understand where your prospective clients are in their awareness journey and then talk to them in a way that appeals to their situation, doesn't overwhelm them, and instead guides them rather than sells to them.

Let's look at the five levels:

- **Unaware**: A person doesn't know they have a problem, or can't yet see the opportunity for change, and it can take a lot of time, energy and effort to move them to the next level.
- **Problem Aware**: A person knows they have a problem, or can see an opportunity for change but doesn't know there are solutions to the outcome they have identified.
- **Solution Aware**: A person discovers that there are solutions, but hasn't chosen one, and is still deciding if they're ready to do the work.
- **Product Aware**: A person is ready to do the work and is looking for a product that matches what they perceive the solution to be. They're trying to work out if your product can help them solve their problem or support them in the change they want to make.
- **Most Aware**: A person has decided they're ready to work with you, they are on the cusp of buying but need to feel supported in taking the first step.

Most people think, and most marketing advice will tell you, to focus on those on the Unaware level, as that is what the big brands do. For a considered purchase, and without an advertising budget of millions, this is often highly ineffective. This is why most marketing doesn't work.

What's more, if you try to take people through these five levels too quickly they get overwhelmed and feel like they're being sold to – nobody likes that and that's not what we're trying to do here. For example:

"Are you feeling stressed? – Buy my 6-week Better Sleep programme!"

This is too fast! If I am feeling stressed then why do I need or want a better sleep programme? Will this help? How? Why?

If you try to close the sale too early, you confuse the client.

It's far better to build curiosity, creating a little tension or an itch to know more. People love to explore and learn about new things, so a better approach would be to take the client on a journey that they can explore at their own pace. This is what the five levels of awareness enable you to do.

The 6-box plan approach in this book enables you to engage your audience and prospective clients - at whatever stage of the journey they're at - with useful content that lets them move to becoming a client at their own pace.

74

Notes:

75

Thanks

It would not have been possible to write this book without the support of many people. I would like to thank my business partner Ben Davis for trusting and supporting me for over 20 years in business and giving me the time and space to write this book. Laurence and Carlos from The Happy Startup School for showing me there is another way to do business and for starting me on the journey that became this book. To Frances Khalastchi for helping me refine the process and language I use in marketing. To Alice Karolina of The Ethical Move for helping me shape my ideas and sparking the movement that caught my attention and inspired me to write this book in the first place. Susan Payton for writing such a great book on storytelling and generously allowing me to share her ideas in this book. Rob Fitzpatrick for helping me believe I could write a book, and all those in the Useful Authors community who helped me distil my ideas and shared such valuable knowledge. And finally, to Dave Foxall, my editor, for helping me to get my ideas out into the world in a way that people can read with a lot fewer spelling mistakes!

76

About the author

Simon Batchelar is a marketing mentor and the co-founder of Five Fathoms, the digital marketing agency they have run for 20 years. During that time, they have transformed over 400 small businesses. Drawing on their experience with freelancers and solopreneurs, Simon developed the proven techniques for more ethical marketing in this book.

Previously in audio production, Simon has also worked with some of the world's biggest brands – including BMW, Ford, Audi, Volvo, IBM, HP, Adobe and GSK – not to mention working on BAFTA and OSCAR award-winning TV series. A career highlight was recording the sound for a documentary, Piano To Zanskar, about an expedition to carry a piano over the Himalayas.

Photo by Roxy Van Der Post

Discover more ethical marketing content at - simonbatchelar.co.uk

Connect with Simon on LinkedIn:

linkedin.com/in/simon-batchelar

Printed in Great Britain
by Amazon

40588994R00155